Passing Through

Passing Through

The End-of-Life Decisions of Lesbians and Gay Men

Jeanette A. Auger

Fernwood Publishing • Halifax, Nova Scotia

Editing: Joanne Richardson
Cover image: Diego Meozzi — Stone Pages (www.stonepages.com)
Design and production: Beverley Rach
Printed and bound in Canada by: Hignell Printing Limited

A publication of:
Fernwood Publishing
Site 2A, Box 5, 8422 St. Margaret's Bay Road
Black Point, Nova Scotia, B0J 1B0
and 324 Clare Avenue
Winnipeg, Manitoba, R3L 1S3
www.fernwoodbooks.ca

Fernwood Publishing Company Limited gratefully acknowledges
the financial support of the Department of Canadian Heritage,
the Nova Scotia Department of Tourism and Culture
and the Canada Council for the Arts for our publishing program.

National Library of Canada Cataloguing in Publication

Auger, Jeanette A., 1945-
Passing through : end of life decisions of gays, lesbians, gay men /
Jeanette A. Auger.

Includes bibliographical references.
ISBN 1-55266-117-2

1. Same-sex marriage. 2. Aged gays. 3. Gays—Death. I. Title.

HQ1033.A84 2003   306.84'8   C2003-903820-3

Contents

For Elvi Whittaker
Teacher, mentor, and friend, who, when I was a student at the University of British Columbia, always told me to "write about the gay community" and to "write about what you know." So I did.

Acknowledgments

I want to offer my deepest thanks to all of the lesbians and gay men whose experiences inform this work. Without your support and input this book would not have been possible. As well, I want to thank the creators of the following Web sites and publications for their support and encouragement, and their belief that this was important work: Gay Canada, Equality for Gays and Lesbians Everywhere (EGALE), Same-Sex Marriage, The Nova Scotia Rainbow Action Project (NSRAP), Older Wiser Lesbians (OWLS), and *Wayves*.

My publisher, Errol Sharpe (and his staff), has always encouraged any book ideas that I have presented to him. In 2003 Fernwood Books celebrates its twenty-fifth anniversary. Errol's courage and determination to succeed as a small independent publisher in Canada has proven extremely successful, and I congratulate him, Bev, Larissa, and all the other good folk who work at Fernwood. And I thank them for their work on my behalf.

Joanne Richardson, who edited this book, made numerous helpful suggestions throughout the journey from research to writing. I am thankful for her insight, friendship, and love. I also thank Brenda Conroy for bringing her proof reading skills to the final pages. My friends Nicki and Sue Perkins and Karla Henderson were particularly helpful in assisting me to go forward with this research, and I thank them for that.

My partner, Susan Riordan, has been my biggest supporter, as well as lover and companion, throughout this journey, and, as usual, I give her my thanks.

Introduction

Helfer (cited in Wintermute and Andenaes 2001: 734) has noted that, since Denmark became the first nation in the world to enact a registered partnership law, in 1989, "same-sex couples in more than a dozen countries have achieved, if not the right to marry, then at least some meaningful slice of the rights, privileges, and responsibilities that married and unmarried heterosexual couples have long enjoyed." During the 1980s and 1990s court challenges (especially to the Charter of Rights and Freedoms) have been used to advance the equality rights of lesbians and gay men in Canadian society. In June 2001 Nova Scotia became the third province to pass legislation (Bill 75) to allow same-sex couples to legally register their relationships. Manitoba and Quebec passed similar legislation in 2001 and 1998, respectively. The registered domestic partnership certification (commonly known as RDP) permits same-sex partners to register their relationships so that they may have legal rights and obligations similar to those of common-law heterosexual couples. Bill 75 and its federal counterpart, Bill C23, cover sixty-eight federal and provincial statutes involving some twenty departments, ranging from the Income Tax Act, to the Canadian Pension Plan, to the Old Age Security Act, to the Criminal Code. (For a more detailed description of this legislation see Fisher, Lahey, and Arron 2000.)

Even though the past forty years have witnessed a number of remarkable legal developments in Canada with regard to same-sex benefits, as Demczuk et al. (2002: ix) note, "Without wishing to minimize the importance of these breakthroughs, we must observe that they have for the most part been the results of legal challenges rather than the expression of political will on the part of the federal and provincial governments to eliminate discrimination." In Canada, unlike in Scandinavian countries, the Netherlands, and Belgium, legislative changes that benefit same-sex couples have been reactive rather than proactive statements of government recognition.

Prior to these legislative changes we have been denied access to most of the rights and responsibilities that opposite-sex partners have enjoyed and taken for granted. The consequences of this unequal and discriminatory treatment have often been devastating for us. As the authors of *Registering as Domestic Partners* note:

> Lesbians and gay men have been prevented from seeing our long-term partners in the hospital and excluded from decision-making when our partners were incapacitated. We have been denied access to easy and secure means of adopting our partners' children. Our employers may not have provided health insurance that covered our partners or, if our employers did, we were required to pay taxes on the cost of that insurance that employees who were provided insurance coverage for their legal spouses didn't have to pay. If our partners were killed, our right to sue for their loss was in doubt. (Lambda Legal Defense and Education Center 2002: 3)

Whereas the above refers to the importance of registered domestic partnership legislation in California, most of what it says is also true for Canadian lesbians and gay men.

In *Passing Through* I discuss the end-of-life decisions of some lesbians and gay men who live in Nova Scotia, Ontario, British Columbia, Alberta, and New Brunswick in light of newly passed federal and provincial legislation aimed at (theoretically) advancing our equality rights. The extensive literature and research on end-of-life issues in Canada focuses primarily on the needs of heterosexuals, with very little mention being made of how these issues affect lesbians and gay men. When mention of our needs is made at all, it is normally with respect to the end-of-life, health-related treatment options available to gay men with HIV/AIDS infections (see, for example, Singer, Martin, and Kelner 1999; Martin, Thiel, and Singer 2002; Singer et al. 1997). According to Singer, Martin, and Kelner (1999: 168), from a patient's perspective quality end-of-life care includes five domains: "receiving adequate pain and symptom management, avoiding inappropriate prolongation of dying, achieving a sense of control, relieving burden, [sic] and strengthening relationships with loved ones." Part of being in control and strengthening relationships with loved ones includes making appropriate decisions and arrangements for the passing on of assets and other property to one's same-sex partner.

Because many lesbians and gay men still choose to remain "closeted" they are unaware of the implications of *not* making end-of-life decisions, such as not having access to decision making around: (1) how, where, and by whom partners may be cared for; (2) funeral and final disposition arrangements after death; (3) loss of rights to pensions, residences, custody of children, and so on. As well, individuals who are in the closet may experience what Doka (1989) has identified as "disenfranchised grief." This type of grief occurs when persons cannot openly acknowledge their loss and, therefore, do not receive social and familial support for their mourning.

Some people who choose to live openly as lesbians or gay men are insufficiently aware of the need to make end-of-life decisions and of the impact of the obligations as well as the benefits of the Nova Scotia Law Reform Act, 2000 (Bill 75), and the federal Modernization of Benefits and Obligations Act, 2000 (Bill C23). I am particularly concerned with the ways in which Bill 75 and Bill C23 affect such decisions, especially with regard to living wills, power of attorney, health guardianship, matrimonial property, estate planning, pre-planning funerals, organ donations, child custody, access and support in the case of death, pensions, and any taxes payable on death.

Methodology

I gathered material for *Passing Through* by reviewing and critiquing both Canadian and international literature concerning the end-of-life decisions of lesbians and gay men. This literature included government publications, books, magazine and journal articles, and items posted on various Web sites. A series of five focus group meetings was held in the Province of Nova Scotia; a questionnaire (see Appendix) was distributed on-line via Gay Canada, Equality for Gays and Lesbians Everywhere (EGALE), and Same-Sex Marriage. I also sent this questionnaire, via e-mail (eighteen) and Canada Post (forty), to lesbians and gay men in British Columbia and Ontario, thus relying on the snowball technique. I held on-line discussions with lesbians and gay men throughout Nova Scotia and other regions of Canada. As well, I gathered information through such lesbian and gay organizations as Gay Canada, EGALE, the Nova Scotia Rainbow Connection, Older Wiser Lesbians (OWL), the Canadian Gay and Lesbian Studies

Association, and Same-Sex Marriage; I asked about opinions and practices with respect to Bills 75 and C23 and whether or not this legislation had been seen to influence end-of-life decisions. *Wayves*, a newspaper targetted at lesbians, gays, bisexual, and transgendered persons in Atlantic Canada, ran the questionnaire in its March 2003 issue. In all, 163 people responded to the questionnaire, participated in the focus groups, and/or returned questionnaires through the mail.

During the data-gathering and writing processes I explored whether or not and why lesbians and gay men have made end-of-life decisions for themselves, their partners, and their important ones. My intention is to provide lesbians and gay men with the opportunity to gain access to information that may assist them in making informed end-of-life choices. I was able to provide such information in the focus group sessions as well as by addressing questions from respondents to the questionnaire. I now hope that *Passing Through* will make this information more widely available. In order to protect the privacy of those who shared with me their experiences and opinions, the names of all of those who responded to the questionnaire and who participated in the focus groups have been changed.

Chapter One

The History of Same-Sex Legislation

International

O ver the past two decades there have been some major milestones in international legislation aimed at granting equality rights to same-sex partners, especially in Europe and North America. These rights have fallen into three categories: (1) same-sex marriage, (2) registered domestic partnerships, and (3) cohabitation. As Herman (1994: 4) notes, "the positive legal recognition of lesbian and gay sexuality (as opposed to negative criminal law constructions) promotes feelings of self-worth, citizenship and community identity." The following timeline provides a brief overview of which countries have granted such rights over the past twenty years:

1987   **Sweden** accorded limited recognition to same-sex, cohabiting couples in its family law legislation.

1989   Under the Danish Registered Partnership Act, **Denmark** was the first country to legally recognize same-sex partnerships. However, as Merin (2002: 357) notes, **South Africa** was the first country in the world to "enshrine lesbian and gay rights in its constitution."

1992   **New Zealand** passed legislation granting same-sex benefits.

1993   **Norway** passed same-sex registered partnership legislation.

1994   **Australia** passed the Domestic Relationship Act.

1995   **Sweden** passed laws to adopt the Danish model of registered partnerships.
       Hungary amended its Civil Code so that the definition of partners included two people living together in an emotional and economic community in the same household without being married.

1996	**Iceland** passed a law on confirmed cohabitation for same-sex partners.
1998	**Austria** changed its criminal code to recognize the legal rights of persons living with each other in a community of life.

2000

January **New Zealand** provided broad-based recognition of same-sex rights to estates, property, spousal maintenance, and child adoption.

May The State of **Vermont** was the first in the United States of America to enact the Civil Union Act, providing same-sex couples with rights, benefits, and responsibilities similar to those provided to heterosexuals. Other American states also offering domestic partnerships are Arizona, Arkansas, California, Colorado, Connecticut, District of Columbia, Florida, Georgia, Hawaii, Illinois, Indiana, Iowa, Louisiana, Maine, Maryland, Massachusetts, Michigan, Missouri, New Jersey, New York, North Carolina, Oregon, Pennsylvania, Vermont, Washington, and Wisconsin. (For further information on same-sex legislation in the Unites States, see "Summary of States, Cities, and Counties which Prohibit Discrimination Based on Sex Orientation," Lambda Legal on-line < http:// www.lambdalegal.org>.)[1]

July The State of **Hawaii** granted same-sex couples the right to register as domestic partners.

September Dutch law was the first to allow same-sex couples to marry, and the **Netherlands** provides us with the same rights as those granted to heterosexuals when it comes to adoption.

November **Germany** enacted registered partnership legislation at the federal level.

2001 **France, Israel, Portugal**, and **Spain** introduced same-sex registered partnerships legislation.
Scotland was the first country in the United Kingdom to grant same-sex benefits to lesbians and gay men.

2002

March After several bills were introduced into the Finnish Parliament (in 1993, 1996, and 1999, respectively) and were subjected to much debate, **Finland** approved the Registered Partnership Act.

May   The newly elected president of **Brazil** endorsed a proposal to legalize same-sex unions.

September The State of Tasmania in **Australia** agreed to recognize domestic partnerships and, in so doing, made its legislation the most progressive in gay family law in the country.

November The **Belgian** Senate approved same-sex marriages and is awaiting approval from the lower house of Parliament.

2003

February **Belgium** becomes the second country in the world to legally recognize gay marriages. However, unlike the Netherlands, the Belgian Parliament will not allow same-sex married couples to adopt children.

April   The City of Buenos Aires and Rio Negro province in **Argentina** made history when they became the first areas in Latin America to recognize same-sex unions.

(Adapted from Wintermute and Andenaes 2001; Wood 2002; Uk.gay.com 1999-2003; 365Gay.com 1999-2003; and Merin 2002.)[2]

National

The following Canadian provinces have passed legislation granting benefits to same-sex partners:

British Columbia	1992
Quebec	1999
Yukon Territories	1998
Ontario	1999
New Brunswick	2000
Newfoundland and Labrador	2000
Nova Scotia	2000
Manitoba	2001
Saskatchewan	2001
Prince Edward Island	2002

(For more information on the specific pieces of legislation, see Gordon 2001.)

Even though, in 2002, the Alberta Law Reform Institute produced a position paper recommending that same-sex partners in Alberta receive recognition of their relationships, legislation has yet to be put forward. As of June 2003 neither the new territory of Nunavut nor the Northwest Territories has legalized same-sex benefits (Wood 2002). By 2002 all provinces and territories, except those noted above, had brought in same-sex legislation.

All of the provincial legislation passed so far uses a rights-based ideology to justify granting same-sex couples equal opportunities and obligations. For the most part, the purpose of changing these federal and provincial laws has been to include same-sex conjugal partners within the definition of "common-law partner." According to the federal government, common-law partners are "two persons, regardless of sex, who cohabit in a conjugal relationship and have done so for a period of at least 12 months" (Canada Customs and Revenue Agency 2000). In provinces that have the a registered domestic partnership law or equivalent (Nova Scotia, Manitoba, and Quebec) or Ontario and British Columbia, which have same-sex marriage, the term "spouse" has been amended to include same-sex partners.

Each year taxpayers who can afford to do so may contribute a percentage of their income to a registered retirement pension plan (RRSP) or, in Quebec, a registered partnership program (RPP), in order to decrease their annual taxes and to save for their retirement. Under Bill C23 a same-sex surviving spouse is entitled to this income at the death of her or his partner. As well, it is now possible for same-sex partners to contribute to a spousal RRSP/RPP if their partner is unable, or unwilling, to contribute in her/his own name. As well, under Bill C23 elderly same-sex couples have the opportunity to share Canadian pension retirement benefits, while survivors are eligible for survivor benefits. With regard to changes to the Old Age Security Program (OASP), when benefits are determined it is now possible to include both same-sex partners' incomes (or lack thereof). The Guaranteed Income Supplement (GIS), which is an assistance program for those with low retirement incomes (especially those who do not receive the Old Age Security Supplement known as Spouse's Allowance), is now available to same-sex couples. (For more information about all federal benefits now available to same-sex couples, see Demczuk et al. 2002.

Federal and Provincial Legislation
Covering Same-Sex Relationships

Many terms are used to designate the legal status established by relationship registration initiatives at provincial, national, and international levels. Most are used interchangeably, and they include the following: registered domestic partnerships, domestic partnerships, registered partnerships, life partnerships, civil unions, legal cohabitation, and unmarried couples. Regardless of the terms used, all refer to the legal processes through which unmarried individuals of the same sex (or, under common law, of the opposite sex) can register their mutually dependent relationships in order to gain official state and societal recognition. The Law Commission of Canada (2002: 2) states that "'partnership' is a commonly used word referring to personal relationships and is, therefore, an accurate representation of the interdependent relationships that are the subject of registration methods." They further note that "the term 'registration' aptly covers the fact that all the models reviewed are opt-in schemes, that is, they require partners to identify themselves to the relevant authorities either through registration or the issuance of a licence" (2).

Theoretically, except with regard to marriage (other than in the Netherlands and Belgium), registering one's lesbian- or gay-partnered relationship provides an individual with the same legal rights, benefits, and obligations as accrue to heterosexual couples. These rights include civil rights (such as the right not to have a spouse testify against one in a court of law), social rights (such as those regarding adoption and child custody issues), and economic rights (such as the right to file joint income tax returns, share pension credits, and contribute to spousal registered retirement programs). However, even though these legislative changes provide some rights to lesbian and gay couples, they nonetheless perpetuate discrimination against same-sex couples, for, as Lahey (1999: 244-45) so eloquently points out:

> Whatever the political motivations behind these changes might be, the legislative regimes all have two things in common. First, all of these new legislative structures perpetuate discrimination on the basis of sexuality to some extent or another. ... Second, none of the legislative regimes extend any of the core incidents of marriage to lesbian and gay couples (except in Nova Scotia through the segregated device of registered domestic partnerships).

Aside from the concerns raised by Lahey, such legislation is also jurisdictionally flawed in that it is not transferable from province to province as many statutes do not recognize non-married couples as "spouses." Also, many would argue that it is discriminatory to suggest that the only legitimate form of relationship between two people is that between individuals who are married.

In Nova Scotia any two persons over the age of nineteen, ordinarily resident in that province, and not married or involved in any other domestic partnership may complete a witnessed declaration form stating their intention to become registered domestic partners, pay a fee of twenty dollars, and thus become registered domestic partners. At the time of application couples are also required to provide proof of age, residency, divorce certificates (if applicable), and death certificates (if widowed). They must also complete a signed declaration of domestic partnership, which must be witnessed by one or more persons. (For additional information visit the Department of Vital Statistics for the Government of Nova Scotia on-line at <http://www.gov.ns.ca/snsmr/vstat/certificates/domestic.stm>.)

Once registered as domestic partners, same-sex couples are entitled to a variety of legal benefits deriving from sixty-eight statutes covering some twenty government departments. These benefits include those relating to immigration, pensions and RRSPs, medical benefits, any taxes payable on death, property rights, child custody and adoption, labour laws (regarding sick-leave benefits), custodial rights, and child tax benefits, among others. (For a complete list of statutes affected, please go to the Department of Justice, Canada, Web site at <http://canada.justice.gc.ca/en/news/nr/2000/doc_25021.html> or see Gordon 2001).

The legislative statutes that have a bearing on end-of-life issues for same-sex couples include the following: Canada Pension Plan; Canadian Forces Superannuation Act; Defence Services Pension Continuation Act; Garnishment, Attachment, and Pension Diversion Act; Government Employees Compensation Act; Health Act; Income Tax Act; Indian Act; Members of Parliament Retiring Allowance Act; Old Age Security Act; Pension Act; Pensions Benefits Division Act; Pension Funds Societies Act; Public Pensions Reporting Act; Public Service Superannuation Act; Royal Canadian Mounted Police Pension Continuation Act; Special Retirement Arrangements Act; Supplementary Retirement Benefits Act; Veterans Insurance Act; Vital Statistics Act; War Veterans Allowance Act; and the Wills Act. Under all of these acts the term "spouse" now also refers to same-sex partners as well as to those in common-law relationships. Under the Canada Pension Plan the surviving spouse in a same-sex relationship may qualify for survivor's benefits based on their spouse's contributions to the plan. These changes provide that, in similar circumstances as an opposite-sex couple, the surviving partner in a same-sex common-law relationship would qualify for the same benefits. In a telephone conversation with the Department of Vital Statistics for the Province of Nova Scotia on 22 March 2003, I was informed that 153 couples had chosen to declare themselves as registered domestic partners. Even though no records of the sexual orientation of the registrants is kept, the spokeswoman in the registry office believes that most who have registered to date are in same-sex relationships.

It is commonly believed that the number of lesbians and gay men in the Canadian (or any other) population is one in ten (see, for example, Compas Opinion and Market Research 2000; Michael et al. 1994). Although I doubt that this figure will ever truly be known, as sexual preference is not necessarily a fixed entity and people's self-identity may not correspond with their behaviour, studies asking people about sexual orientation consistently show that individuals who identify themselves as heterosexual also admit to having same-sex fantasies, attractions, and relationships (e.g., Michael et al. 1994; Faulkner and Cranston 1998; Kinsey, Pomeroy, and Martin 1948; Bohan 1996; and Money 1988; among others). Nonetheless, the number of individuals who have thus far chosen to register their relationships in Nova Scotia seems very low. Discussions with friends and acquaintances suggest that there are several reasons for this, including the unwillingness of lesbians and gay men to declare their sexual preference for fear of homophobic reactions from their families or co-workers. As a lesbian couple working for the military noted, "We would love to do the RDP thing but we don't want to jeopardize our jobs or have our families find out. How do you know that they [the government] won't make that stuff public?" (personal communication, December 2002).

A friend who has been conducting research into why lesbians would want to formally register their relationships noted that, in her focus groups, many with whom she spoke did not want to acquire RDPs because they did not want the government to interfere in how they chose to conduct their relationships. As well, she noted that lesbians chose their lifestyle in order to break away from heterosexual norms about how to construct relationships and that, by registering them with the government, not only were they following heterosexual rules but they were also allowing the government to determine how their relationships would be conducted (Mellet 2003).

Related to the issue of whether or not lesbians and gay men chose to legally register their relationships is the issue of identifying same-sex relationships on the Canadian Census. The 2001 census was the first in Canada to include a question regarding same-sex relationships. At that time only 34,200 same-sex couples were counted. Gay rights advocates argue that many lesbians and gay men (especially those living in rural areas) did not answer this question truthfully because they did not trust the government with this sort of information (Thompson 2002). The only other countries to include a question on same-sex common-law relationships in their census information are New Zealand (in 1996) and the United States (in 1990 and 2000).

On 30 January 2003 Statistics Canada announced that it would conduct a national survey to ask people if they are gay, lesbian, or bisexual. In 2004 the Canadian Community Health Study will survey 130,000 Canadians over the telephone. However, John Fisher, former executive director of EGALE Canada, suggested that many will not respond truthfully to the survey. He argued that, for example, "if it's a teenager living at home with his or her parents who has not yet disclosed their sexual orientation to their family, it is unlikely that they're going to disclose it to a government statistician" (cited in Sui 2003a).

Many gay activists argue that it is important for lesbians and gay men to register relationships in both the census and in provincial jurisdictions in order to be recognized and counted as fully functioning families whose rights, obligations, and needs are the same as those of heterosexual cohabiting couples.

The world's first class-action lawsuit against government discrimination towards lesbian, gay, bisexual, and transgendered people is currently being pursued in Toronto. The suit involves people whose partners died between 1985 and 1998. The federal government enacted legislation in

1999 recognizing gay and lesbian families and backdated the cut-off for survivor benefits to 1998. But the suit says that the actual date should have been 1985, when gays and lesbians were first included in the Canadian Constitution. According to Sui (2003b: 1), "The lawsuit also alleges that while the federal government and its agencies collect Canada Pension Plan contributions from all working Canadians regardless of their sexual orientation, it does not provide equal survivor benefits on that basis."

Because in the mid-1980s so many men were losing their life-long partners to AIDS, and because they were not legally entitled to survivor benefits, the necessity of either registering relationships or making legal end-of-life decisions became paramount in the lesbian and gay community. It should be noted that, although lesbians are not at high risk for contracting AIDS, many of us have friends, brothers, sons, ex-husbands, nephews, uncles, and so on who have or have had this disease. Many lesbians work in the caring professions (e.g., medicine, nursing, social work, counselling, spiritual care, etc.) and with gay men who have AIDS. Further, many lesbians identify themselves as members of the lesbian/gay community, and many have been involved in HIV/AIDS organizations since their inception. For all of these reasons, the AIDS pandemic has caused lesbians as well as gay men to think about their own mortality and their decisions around end-of-life care.

Update

Since the completion of this manuscript in May 2003, two events have occurred that may change the legal status of same-sex marriages in this country. On Tuesday, 10 June 2003, the Ontario Court of Appeal unanimously ruled that the exclusion of lesbians and gay men from the institution of marriage was unconstitutional and, therefore, illegal. In bringing forward this decision the Ontario court agreed with earlier decisions made by the Quebec Superior Court (June 2002), the Ontario Superior Court (October 1999), and the British Columbia Court of Appeal (February 2003), all of which stated that not allowing same-sex partners to marry was illegal. The decision of the Ontario Court of Appeal came into effect immediately, with the result that the definition of marriage in Ontario is now "the voluntary union for life of two persons at [sic] the exclusion of all others" (Makin 2003: 1). On 8 July 2003, British Columbia became the second Canadian province to legalize gay marriage when the BC Court of Appeal ruled that it was lifting a one-year moratorium on gay marriage.

Needless to say, while lesbians and gay men celebrated these decisions, others did not. Indeed, newspapers, magazines, and television and radio talk shows included comments from those not at all supportive of this legal decision. We are hearing all the familiar arguments — arguments suggesting that the decision has "devalued the institution of marriage" (Rogusky 2003: A7).

The onus is now on the federal government to bring all of its laws into line with this ruling. On Friday, 13 June 2003, NDP Member of Parliament Svend Robinson presented a motion to the House of Commons Justice Committee insisting that the federal government support the Ontario ruling. This motion passed by one vote.

On 17 June 2003 an all-party committee of the House of Commons agreed not to appeal either the Ontario decision or those made in Quebec and British Columbia (Lunman 2003: 1). On 17 July 2003 Justice Minister Martin Couchon presented a one-page draft bill to the Supreme Court of Canada recommending that the definition of marriage now read: " The lawful union of two persons at the exclusion of all others." As well, the Supreme Court is being asked to decide on three main issues related to this bill. These are 1) Is the draft consistent with the Charter of Rights and Freedom's inclusion of sexuality; 2) Does the draft go far enough in protecting the constitutional rights of religions from being compelled to perform same-sex marriages, contrary to their beliefs; and 3) Does the proposed change fall within the legislative authority of Parliament (and if not, in what particular way and to what extent). Since this bill has been made public, the Canadian Alliance Party and several Christian churches have vowed to fight and defeat this bill. The story continues ...

Notes

1. While there have been many advances towards gay and lesbian rights in the United States, it is also noteworthy that, between January and April 2003, several states have had such rights removed (e.g., Nashville [Tennessee], 5 February; Minnesota, 18 February; Des Moines [Iowa], 15 April; Colorado, 24 April; Virginia Technical School, March 14). For details, see 365.Gay.com/NewsContent.

2. On 23 April 2003, The United Nations began discussions on a bill introduced

by Brazil, with support from various countries (including members of the European Union, Canada, New Zealand, and South Africa), that would recognize homosexual human rights (see Uk.gay.com, 22 April 2003). The United States decided to abstain from voting for this bill. Over seventy countries have a complete ban on homosexuality, with sentences ranging from "imprisonment, to public flogging and death. In seven nations, same-sex relations are punishable by execution. These are Chechnya, Iran, Iraq, Mauritania, Saudi Arabia, Sudan and Yemen" ("Historical First Vote on the Rights of Lesbians, Gay and Bisexual People," Uk.gay.com, 22 April 2003).

Chapter Two

End-of-Life Issues

There are several interconnected end-of-life issues that affect all individuals, regardless of their sexual preference. They include the right to self-determination, being able to communicate one's wishes and concerns to important ones, having the necessary information regarding the withholding/withdrawal of medical care, deciding where to die, making funeral and final disposition arrangements, making legal decisions (e.g., regarding living wills, powers of attorney, etc.), appointing a health guardian, and so on.

The Lambda Legal Defense and Education Fund notes that it is an "absolute necessity" that lesbians and gay men of any age engage in advance planning and preparation for end-of-life decisions: "If you do not have a written plan in place the law directs that your property after death — and, in many cases, the power to make decisions about your health, welfare and finances if you become incapacitated — will be in the hands of your biological relatives. Your wishes — and your closest relationships — may be ignored" (Gewirtzman 2000: n.p.). Even though it is important for all couples to make end-of-life decisions, because of a lack of legal protection and entrenched homophobic attitudes, it is especially important for lesbian and gay male couples to do so.

The Right to Self-Determination

Being able to play a role in our own health care decisions (e.g., being informed of diagnoses and their consequences, treatment options, medical directives, and the necessity of appointing health guardianship in the event that we are unable to speak for ourselves) as well as in the preparation of living and ethical wills enables us to come to terms with our illnesses in ways that allow us to feel that we have some say in the decisions that directly affect end-of-life issues. Being able to include our partners in such matters enables us to know that they (and others important to us) are comfortable with and supportive of our needs, and we of theirs.

Communicating Needs

The ability to effectively communicate end-of-life needs with partners, other important ones (including friends, family members, care providers [both professionals and volunteers], spiritual advisors, legal representatives, funeral directors, etc.) enhances an individual's feelings of self-determination and of being in control of her/his circumstances. If a death is unexpected or accidental, having discussed end-of-life wishes (including organ donations) with partners and other important ones will ensure that our final wishes are respected.

For many lesbians and gay men who are not open about their relationships due to fears of homophobic reactions, choosing to remain in the closet forces them to deny the existence of their partners and/or to trivialize the extent of their relationships. If this is the case at the end of a terminal illness, then the individual loses the comfort, support, and closeness of the person she/he most needs.

A lesbian couple of my acquaintance (names are pseudonymous) had been together for almost twenty years when Gwen was diagnosed with cancer. She chose not to inform her family or the medical personnel responsible for her care of her long-term same-sex relationship for fear of not being accepted (or being treated differently) due to her sexual preference. As a result of this, her partner, Kate, was not recognized as the key person in her life when it came to treatment decisions, powers of attorney, whether she could die in their home or in a palliative care unit, after-death arrangements, and so on. After Gwen died, her obituary identified Kate as a "special friend." In conversation, Kate expressed her concern that they had not been more open with family and friends about the nature of their relationship (in fact, they went out of their way to ensure that their families would not know about it), and she felt very strongly the lack of recognition accorded to their long-term relationship. Kate spoke about the fact that, at work, she couldn't talk about her loss, or get support for it, in the ways that were open to her heterosexual colleagues. As well, after Gwen's death her family wanted to remove some of the couple's possessions, claiming that, as the two women were "just friends," it seemed unlikely that they would have jointly owned paintings, other artwork, crafts, and so on.

Other than information found on the Lambda legal Web site, I was unable to find any written material that dealt with the need for lesbians and gay men to communicate their end-of-life needs with others. However, Judy Small, an Australian lesbian/feminist folksinger, sings about the differences in the experiences of heterosexual women and their lesbian counterparts when it comes to losing a partner to death. I quote the song, "No Tears for the Widow," in full:

I never saw my mother cry until the night my father died
Married nearly thirty years and the dying had been hard
I remember how the family came to share the grief the tears the pain
And how her friends all gathered round and all the black-rimmed cards

The funeral was a large affair, the civic fathers all were there
And mother held up stoically, she never shed a tear
But everyone there understood that she had entered widow-hood
And life would never be the same, her status now was clear

And there were tears for the widow, tears for the widow
For the woman who had lost her love and must carry on alone
And mother now writes 'widow' in the space on all the forms
It's part of her identity, like her grey hair and her name

My friend Amelia lost her love to cancer's slow and painful glove
The dying was no easier than my father's was back then
No black-rimmed cards came to her door, her grief and anguish all ignored
Except of course for closest friends who tried to understand

Her lover was described by all as a single woman living well
A tragic loss for family, taken well before her time
When Amy left the funeral home she travelled to their house alone
And sat among familiar things and wept into the night

And there were no tears for the widow, no tears for the widow
For the woman who had lost her love and must carry on alone
And Amy still writes 'single' in the space on all the forms
But she rages at the lie it tells and the loss that it ignores

And who can tell how many women live their lives in shadows
Unrecognised, unsympathised, unseen and disallowed
Who've lost not only lovers, but often hearth and home
For 'marriage' is a special word and only meant for some

And there are no tears for the widows, no tears for the widows
For the women who've lost lovers and must carry on alone
And life goes on but for them there is no space on any form
Yes 'marriage' is a special word and only meant for some
(Small 1999)

Even though there is increased recognition in the field of palliative care and hospice work for the right of the terminally ill and/or bereaved person to communicate her/his experiences and feelings, there is still a long way to go when it comes to recognizing the rights of same-sex partners. In a recent study conducted in Montreal, Brotman, Ryan, and Cormier of the McGill School of Social Work found that discrimination threatens the health of gay elders and that this, in turn, leads to their being afraid of the health system in general — including the services that are provided for end-of-life care (e.g., palliative care facilities, which are usually located within hospital settings).

> Many gay and lesbian elders who experienced the pervasive social stigma that existed prior to the advent of the gay liberation movement maintain a sense of extreme caution with respect to whether or not societal attitudes have really changed and this has an impact on the ways in which they access health services. In light of this reality, the possibility of one day having to be reliant on the health care system, on a nursing home facility or any other social institution understandably provokes anxiety and fear in aging lesbians and gay men. (Brotman, Ryan, and Cormier 2003:76)

According to this study, because of their fear of homophobic health personnel, many older lesbians and gay men are delaying seeking treatment, and this has consequences for their ability to seek appropriate end-of-life care. It also points to the need for them to make their wishes known to their important ones.

Withholding/Withdrawal of Medical Treatment

In Nova Scotia (other Canadian provinces have similar legislation under different names), the Medical Consent Act, 1988, allows adults to appoint a "proxy" — someone who is authorized to give consent to, or directions regarding, medical treatment if the person appointing her/him ends up being no longer capable of giving consent her/himself. Under this act an individual also has the legal right to withdraw from treatment regimens, even though medical personnel may strenuously object. As well, s/he or her/his proxy can request that specific medical treatment be withheld. Information about treatment decisions is normally included in living wills or advance directives. Even though these documents involve legal decisions, as Dr. Peter Singer (Singer et al. 1999: 9) of the Centre of Bioethics at the University of Toronto points out: "Advance care planning is not about legislation, lawyers and doctors, but rather about relationships, communications and families. Government and professional groups could do much to support the process of advance care planning."

Although living wills are not legally binding in Canada at present, Nova Scotia, Manitoba, Newfoundland, British Columbia, Quebec, and Ontario recognize advance health care directives that provide well thought out instructions to medical personnel regarding which treatments a patient would choose in specific health circumstances (e.g., cancer, Alzheimer's, strokes, severe head injuries, and so on). Alberta, New Brunswick, and the Northwest Territories are considering such directives.

Deciding Where to Die

Even though the majority of Canadians die in institutions such as hospitals, nursing homes, palliative care units, and hospices (where the latter are available), it is important to discuss with our partners where we would choose to die. When I ask the students in my sociology of death and dying classes where they would prefer to die, the vast majority of them say "at home in my bed." However, depending upon both the resources available within an individual's social network and the services available within her/his community, this option may not always be a viable one. Choosing to die at home is an option if one has enough money to pay for professional respite care services, thus allowing the primary caregiver a break from what is normally a twenty-four-hours-a-day, seven-days-a-week task, or if one has a large enough network of friends to assist with the care-giving tasks. However, not all homes are suitably equipped; nor, for that matter, are all individuals. These decisions concerning where a person would prefer to die are important ones, and partners should make them together.

Making Funeral Arrangements

Lesbians and gay men often talk about their desire to have funeral directors who are sensitive to and supportive of their same-sex relationships. A gay male friend started up a cremation service in Nova Scotia precisely because our community lacked such services. As John (a pseudonym) told me while I was touring his facility last year:

> So many of us were truly pissed off at the ways we were being looked at and treated by funeral directors, especially friends whose partners were dying of AIDS, that I decided that we needed a place where we could go and be honest about our relationships without having some homophobic guys looking at us as if we were freaks. I now want to find a space so that we can have our own cemetery or burial plots too. Where our headstones could say stuff like, "Here lies John, beloved partner of Pete." (Personal communication, May 2002)

As well as funeral/cremation services, coffins and urns tend to be made locally by lesbians and gay men. Last year in my sociology of death and dying class a local coffin maker and a woman who manufactures hand-carved cremation urns, both lesbians, gave presentations in which they talked about the fact that most of their business comes from members of the gay and lesbian community who prefer to deal with providers of service who understand and can relate to their needs without judgment or prejudice. As well as a need for regular funerals and celebration of life services, there is also a need to make advance decisions regarding funerals by pre-paying for them. As one informant on a Web site (Gay Canada, <http://www.gaycanada.com> February 27/03) noted: "We are very concerned that Joe's family would contest any arrangement we want to make about funerals, especially as they are so religious and so down on our relationship. So we both decided to pre-plan everything, that way we know we will get the type of funeral services *we* want" (emphasis in original).

Another concern raised by lesbians and gay men with partners or friends who are terminally ill has to do with finding gay-friendly spiritual advisors willing to provide counselling and to perform religious services at funerals and (more commonly) celebrations of life. Even though larger Canadian provinces now have churches/synagogues/places of worship that cater to lesbians and gay men, smaller provinces and rural areas have no such facilities.

Making An Ethical Will

As well as appointing health guardians and providing our partners with powers of attorney if we so wish, there may also be the issue of appointing legal guardians for young children, making decisions about who will be the executors/executrixes of wills, deciding property rights, ensuring that our partners will be adequately provided for in terms of financial assets, and so on. Also, many people are now choosing to leave ethical wills for their important ones, and this is a significant way for lesbians and gay men to leave a legacy to their families, friends, co-workers, and others.

An ethical will allows an individual to share her/his values with those who are left behind. These documents are usually written but can also be produced in the form of video or audio tapes. According to the Web site <http://www.ethicalwill.com/whasin.html.com>, an ethical will reflects the "voice of the heart" in that it is a "love letter to your family." Some common themes found in such wills include "important personal values, important spiritual values, hopes and blessings for future generations, life's lessons and forgiving others and asking for forgiveness." Preparing an ethical will might also be a forum within which lesbians and gay men who are afraid of the consequences of making their relationships public while living can inform their important ones of their sexual preferences and relationships after they have died.

Six years ago a friend who was a gay Roman Catholic priest died of AIDS. Prior to his death he prepared an ethical will in the form of a videotaped presentation in which he discussed his love for men, his relationships with them, and how he was able to reconcile his religiosity with these feelings — feelings that went against the teachings of his church. He wanted this video to be given to his family after his death; he especially wanted his young nephews to know who he had been and that he had chosen to love other men and was proud of the choices he had made in his life. Included in his presentation was a discussion of what he valued in friendships, his love of nature, and his philosophy regarding how to treat others.

End-of-life decisions cover a vast array of topics. Many such decisions have to do with making choices prior to death, others have to do with final disposition and after-death arrangements: all require individuals to be able to share and openly discuss their wishes with those who are most important to them. As Gewirtzman (2000: n.p.) notes: "One day our laws will embrace an expansive definition of family that will provide lesbians and gay men with the same automatic legal safety nets as our non-gay counterparts who can marry. Until then, there is no substitute for careful planning. Get your documents in order, and then take charge of this aspect of your life!"

Chapter Three

Collecting People's Opinions

Sample Size

As of 30 June 2003 I have received communications from 163 people. Twenty-eight participated in focus groups in either Halifax or Wolfville, Nova Scotia; twenty-two returned the questionnaire through Canada Post; seventy-three responded to the questionnaire through Web sites and chat rooms; thirteen completed the questionnaire in the March edition of *Wayves*; and twenty-seven sent e-mail responses to the questionnaire.

I provide a brief statistical breakdown of the responses I received and then go on to discuss them in greater depth, using the informants voices to discuss and analyze the material collected.

Provincial Breakdown of Respondents

Respondents lived in the following provinces:

Alberta	4
British Columbia	11
Nova Scotia	78
New Brunswick	5
Ontario	65

I do not know why gays and lesbians from other provinces did not respond to the questionnaire posted on the Web sites. I did not have personal contacts to whom I could send questionnaires in other regions of the country, and this undoubtedly accounts for some of the skewing.

Not all on-line or mail-in respondents provided their names, although most did. Some gave pseudonyms. All the people in the focus groups provided their names. In what follows, the names of all respondents and focus group participants are pseudonymous.

Sex Differences in Respondents

The number of responses based on sex was fairly even, with 51 percent coming from women and 49 percent coming from men. Interestingly, I received no responses from females through Web sites. In e-mail conversations with the site developers I was informed that more men than women visit such sites, although no one is sure why that might be so.

Ages of Respondents

Respondents ranged in age from eighteen to sixty-eight, with nearly half (43 percent) aged thirty to forty. Of the rest, 48 percent were over forty, and 9 percent were under thirty.

Length of Time in Relationship

Everyone who participated in the data collection process said that they were in same-sex relationships, most of them (67 percent) for more than five years. The shortest length of time given for being in a relationship was one year and three months; the longest was twenty-three years. Many people (23 percent) chose not to respond to this question.

Were Relationships Registered?

Of those respondents who lived in Nova Scotia, the only province among those from which I received responses that has registered domestic partnerships, only 42 percent had registered their relationships. Many reasons were given for this, and they will be discussed later. For now, suffice it to say that those who chose not to register their relationships spoke vehemently about not wanting to, as one informant put it, "heterosize" their relationships.

End-of-Life Decisions

Most respondents (97 percent) agreed that it was important to make end-of-life decisions, and most (76 percent) had done so (this seemed to be especially the case for those who were in RDPs and/or those who indicated their intention to marry if and when such legislation is passed). The types of end-of-life decisions most frequently noted were wills, living wills, medical directives, powers of attorney, and life insurance. Some respondents (28 percent) discussed having joint accounts and joint ownership of property. A few informants (10 percent) were still involved in heterosexual marriages, and their decisions regarding end-of-life plans were complicated by this fact. I shall discuss this issue more fully in Chapter 5.

Reasons for Making End-of-Life Decisions

Many respondents (37 percent) cited planning to register their relationships or to marry as their reasons for making end-of-life decisions. In Nova Scotia lawyers in the gay community frequently provide estate-planning sessions free of charge, and these information sessions caused many couples to choose to make legal arrangements concerning their own or their partners' deaths. Most (69 percent) of the individuals who had made end-of-life decisions had also discussed end-of-life issues — specifically, medical treatment options, funeral/cremation/burial wishes, organ donations, estate planning, and investments. In Canada it is illegal for gay men to donate organs or blood products, and this topic was hotly debated in both focus groups as well as in the questionnaire. I present some of these discussions in Chapter 5. Very few (18 percent) of the respondents had children, but those who did had discussed appointing partners as legal guardians, especially if children had been born as the result of artificial insemination or had been obtained through adoption.

Awareness of the Difficulties Faced by Others

The majority (63 percent) of gay men had heard of lesbians and other gay men having had difficulties at the death of a partner. HIV/AIDS deaths were most frequently mentioned. Not as many lesbians (43 percent) had heard similar stories or had such experiences. Often mentioned was a film entitled *If These Walls Could Talk 2* (Warner Home Box Office 2000). This film consisted of three vignettes, and, in one of them, Vanessa Redgrave stars as one-half of an older, closeted lesbian couple. Her partner dies suddenly, and the house, which they had shared for many years but which was in her partner's name, goes to the deceased woman's relatives. The character played by Redgrave is left with nothing. Many lesbians also talked about the situation faced by Alice B. Toklas, the lifelong partner of American writer Gertrude Stein. Stein's family removed artwork and other valuables the couple had collected together after Gertrude died. Russell (1995) notes that Toklas and Stein were "the most famous lesbian couple in the world" (29), and yet, as Demczuk, Caron, Rose, and Bouchard (2002: 1) point out:

In 1967, over 30 years ago now, Alice B. Toklas, the lifelong companion of the American author Gertrude Stein died in Paris in extreme poverty. Alice acted in turn as secretary, cook and organizer of one of the most glittering literary salons of the day held in the couple's apartment in the rue de Fleurus in Paris. Nonetheless, Gertrude still did not have the courage to use her nimble pen to express her true wishes in her will.

In the lesbian and gay communities, part of our cultural history includes the stories of women like Gertrude and Alice who, in spite of their fame and wealth, did not make the end-of-life decisions that would have ensured that their partners could live out their lives in comfort and security.

Additional Comments

A minority of respondents (14 percent) provided additional comments concerning what they felt should be included in *Passing Through*. These are discussed in Chapter 5. Some noted that being in the focus groups, reading the questionnaire, and discussing the topics on-line provided them with an opportunity to address these topics. For example, Tina, who is from Nova Scotia and in a one-and-a-half-year relationship, said: "We have spent quite a bit of time talking about these issues since we received the survey. It also got us talking about how we see ourselves as lesbians and whether or not we should do more legal stuff around our relationship." And Clare, who is also from Nova Scotia and is in a twelve-year relationship, said: "Talking about your questions has been really helpful to us. We are especially interested because of course we have been taking care of my mum and all the legal stuff has been very complicated. Also, we have our own health conditions to deal with. We are making a New Year's resolution *now* to deal with the legalities of our relationship!"

Chapter Four

The Debate around Registering Same-Sex Relationships

There was a great deal of discussion, especially in the focus groups, concerning whether or not lesbians and gay men ought to register their relationships or to support the ongoing legislative fight for marriage. Interestingly, more men, especially younger men, wanted the right to marry than did women of any age. In 1972 Jesse Bernard suggested that the experience of marriage was very different for women than it was for men. She noted that it was more advantageous for the latter because it provided them with nurturance, physical care, and free domestic and sexual services as well as free child-bearing and child-rearing services (Bernard 1972). Since then, other authors have agreed that "his" and "hers" marriages exist as very different realities (see, for example, McDaniel and Tepperman 2000; Baker 1984; Glenn 1987; Schumm et al. 1996; Pina and Bengston 1995; among others). While this logic may well hold for heterosexual relationships, it does not necessarily hold for gay male relationships. Presumably, in the latter, the relationships would be more equal than would traditional male/female relationships in terms of comparable earnings, nurturance, domestic and sexual services, and so on.

In three of my courses I asked the approximately 120 students (roughly 70 percent female and 30 percent male), whether they would choose to marry or to have less formal relationships. The vast majority of males said that they would prefer a less formal situation (such as a common-law relationship), whereas about 80 percent of the women preferred marriage. When I asked why, given this response, so many men were married I was informed that, as one young man put it, "the girls talk us into marriage, they won't have sex unless we marry them." I asked two colleagues to ask the same question in their classes (which were of similar composition to mine), and they reported similar responses. While it may be true that marriage is more advantageous for heterosexual men than it is for heterosexual women, based on my brief survey few of them (at least those between eighteen and twenty-five years of age) seem to desire it. Why gay men would choose marriage is not clear, although many spoke of a desire to be seen as equal in law to their heterosexual counterparts.

Fewer women than men wanted the right to marry, and many invoked feminist thinking about marriage as a reason for not having anything to do with that particular institution. For example, Joanne and Ev, who are from Ontario and are in a twelve-year relationship, said:

> As feminists we want nothing to do with marriage, and we have preached this to young women always. Marriage ties us down, makes us the property of our husbands, retains patriarchal control of women's bodies, and perpetuates violence against our children and us. Why would any woman in their right mind, straight or gay, want to marry?

Also invoking feminism as an analytic tool for making sense of marriage and, indeed, as a reason for avoiding it, Ann and Chrissie, who are from Nova Scotia and are in an eleven-year relationship, said:

> I don't understand why intelligent women, and especially lesbians, who are supposed to be doing relationships differently than straights, would want the right to marry or to register their relationships. Feminism taught us that we no longer need to be chattel or owned by men for their power and pleasure. Our sisters marched for the right to be free, to be able to vote, to take control of our bodies. Why would women want to have relationships which reproduce patriarchy? Why would they want do this to each other?

Whereas some respondents stressed that their feminist beliefs ran contrary to the concept of same-sex marriage, others explained that they had been or were presently involved in heterosexual marriages and did not want to replicate those relationships in a same-sex situation. As Becky, who is from Nova Scotia and is in a five-year relationship, said:

> We deliberately chose not to register our relationship even though we could have. Ann is still married to her ex and has yet to get a

divorce. Their relationship was a sham, she did everything for him and he held on tight to the purse strings and expected her to do whatever he wanted all the time. When he found out about us, even though he had been screwing around for years, he threatened to keep the kids away from her and "out" her to her boss. We would never want to own each other like that. It's funny, on the surface they had the "normal" marriage thing but there was no love there. Now that there is, we're the ones who are supposed to be "deviant."

Like Becky, many others who had not registered their same-sex relationships spoke of the need to do things "differently" from heterosexuals. As Kate, who is from Nova Scotia and who is in a seven-year relationship, noted:

I have no interest in the state being involved in defining the nature of my relationship or the financial/personal arrangements of how my partner and I wish to support each other. I value and want to be able to talk about and negotiate our own arrangements, and so far we have managed to do that, through both easy and difficult times — living together and not living together.

An unnamed respondent, also from Nova Scotia and in a four-year same-sex relationship, shared Kate's opinion: "Too hetero for me. I prefer to be lesbian-defined. Not mainstream patriarchal."

For lesbians who had previously been married, the idea of registering their same-sex relationships was often seen as problematic. Claire, who is from Nova Scotia and is in a five-year relationship, had this to say:

Well, I did all that marriage stuff before. Why on earth would I want to tie myself down to someone like that again? The whole fascination and wonder of becoming a lesbian was for me to be able to give up all that formal stuff, which is so predetermined. I wanted us to be able to set our own agenda as to how our relationship would work. I don't want to be registered or married. I want the challenge of finding new ways to forge a relationship and be together.

In a similar vein, Heather, who lives in British Columbia and is in an eleven-year relationship, said:

> We were both married before and left those marriages because we found them to be too confining and our needs were not being met. No wonder there is such a high divorce rate in Canada. Marriage is too restrictive for women and men. When we became lovers, after eleven years of being friends, we wanted to do things differently, give each other space, not cling or hold on and live our lives by predetermined rules. If we were to register our relationship somehow that freedom would be diminished and once again we would live normative lives.

The notion of wanting to do things "differently" was invoked by several respondents, mostly women, who often said that they chose to be lesbians in order to be able to live without the restrictions of heterosexual relationships. As well, many spoke about choosing not to register their relationships or to marry because both of these options seemed to threaten the egalitarian nature of their relationships.

In agreement with the concept of avoiding same-sex marriage because it reifies rather than challenges traditional gender roles, Nan Hunter (1991: 25) suggests that the social meaning of the legalization of lesbian and gay marriage, for example, would "be enormously different if legalization resulted from political efforts framed as ending gendered roles between spouses rather than if it were the outcome of a campaign valorizing the institution of marriage, even if the ultimate 'holding' is the same."

Lynn, who is from Nova Scotia and is in a twelve-year relationship, felt that by registering their relationship she and her partner would be moving from a "special minority group" status to what she referred to as a "mainstream privileged" status. She noted further that,

> [by] buying into the acceptable form of relationship [we, as lesbians, would be] selling ourselves and our partners short. I don't want to be another Hollywood/Toronto couple living the perfect movie or television family life. That's too easy. We want a relationship on our own terms, which we work out to suit our

needs and expectations. We live in rural Nova Scotia, we farm, we agree to share the chores and care for our kids. We are monogamous because we choose it, not because it is decreed. If we ever decided to separate we would do what was best for each other and the kids because we believe that we should be fair and decent to one another, not because a piece of paper or a law tells us what we *should* do. We prefer a commitment to equality, not to the status quo!

Clearly, these respondents (as well as others) felt very strongly that to register their relationships would legitimize them in ways that they found highly problematic. They also rejected the notion of normalizing what they had fought so hard to make unique.

Some respondents (11 percent), especially those in the military, were concerned about the lack of portability with regard to RDPs, which are not transferable from province to province. For example, Mike, who lives in Ontario, is a member of the military, and is in a seven-year relationship, said:

> We are both in the army and want to marry so that no matter where we are transferred our relationship will be recognized and we will be seen as "spouses." The RDP thing you have there in Nova Scotia doesn't allow for that so it wouldn't work for us even if Ontario had such rules.

Fisher, Lahey, and Arron (2000: 72) also discuss the issue of the lack of portability of RDPs:

> Another concern with registered domestic partnerships is their lack of portability. Although other jurisdictions might consider them as evidence of the nature of the relationship, it is unlikely that the status would be directly recognized, nor all the rights and obligations that accompany that status. Finally, it is open to question whether domestic partnership registries confer equal status with marriage, or whether by setting up a separate regime, they reinforce inequality of status between married couples and those couples prohibited from marrying.

barbara findley (1997) also notes that lesbians tend to be more critical of the strategies of obtaining the right to marry than are gay men. She thinks that demanding the right to marry is, in certain respects, tantamount to asking the government to become involved by way of establishing a contract regulating

> various material aspects of an intimate relationship between two persons. If this strategy is successful, lesbians may well find themselves bound by laws made for and in the interest of heterosexual men. Findlay [sic] argues that lesbians should instead seek other legal means of ensuring their own models of conjugal life. (findley, cited in Demczuk et al. 2001: 25)

Amy, who is from Ontario and is in an eight-year relationship, saw a struggle within the lesbian and gay community between those who believe that registering relationships and marriage should be an option for same-sex couples and those who do not. In light of the Parliamentary Justice Committee hearings that were taking place across the country during the time of this research, she said:

> Personally I don't need anyone else to tell me how to run a relationship. Especially not homophobic governments. I am very concerned about the split in our community over the marriage issue. Everywhere the parliamentary committee goes they leave a trail of disgruntled people — those who want our relationships sanitized by registration or marriage and those who don't. It is really splitting up the community; but then maybe that was always the plan. Divide and conquer the queers!

Among those who had chosen to register their relationships or who want the right to marry, many invoked the notion of sharing basic human rights with all other Canadians. As Rick, who is from Ontario and is in a four-year relationship, said:

> To me it is a no-brainer. All we are asking for is the same human rights as everyone else: we want to get married and as soon as the law is passed we will. We are in the military and we want to be

recognized as a couple whether we live in Toronto, Calgary, or Halifax. Why should we have to lie in some places where we live, and have no rights, and be freely open in others? What is so threatening about two people of the same-sex loving each other? I just don't get it.

Similarly, John, who is from Alberta and is in a two-year relationship, commented: "Legally and morally it is totally inappropriate that we can live together as spouses in some provinces and not in others. Damn right I want us to be able to register our relationship, and we want to marry as soon as we can."

Another reason that was often raised in response to why couples decided to register their relationships concerned a wish "[to] make a political stand" (Emily and Jane, Nova Scotia, in a twenty-year relationship). Nineteen percent agreed with this opinion. For example, Jan and Amy, who are from Nova Scotia and are in a nine-year relationship, said: "We wanted to legalize our commitment to each other in a formal manner, in front of our families and friends, by getting the RDP. As well we wanted to show to government that we are proud of our relationship." Eric and Brian, who are from Ontario and are in a three-year relationship, commented: "We did this so that I [Eric] would have the same rights and knowledge as heterosexual couples in the military. This will include benefits in the event of the unthinkable, pay increases, and the ability to get a place together."

Andrea and Jill, who are from Nova Scotia and are in a fourteen-and-a-half-year relationship, wanted to register their relationship not only for "political reasons" but also so that their children could see that they were proud of who they are. As Andrea noted:

> We did the registration because we want to politically support the cause for equal rights. We thought that the more people that registered the more it showed we — gays and lesbians — were interested in equal rights; namely, to have the right to marriage. If no one registered we felt it would demonstrate that we had no interest in commitments or gaining rights. We also wanted to take advantage of any legal avenues that would protect our property rights in case of death. We wanted to make sure that our final

wishes [would] be followed and have the legal backing for it. With the baby we wanted to be sure that everything was up front and legal. We don't have any reason to believe our families would not respect our wishes, but we wanted to make sure. And people tend to get very weird after someone dies.

My partner, Susan, and I, who had been together for two and a half years at the time, decided to register our relationship in the summer of 2002. We made this decision because we both felt it important to stand up and be counted among the many lesbians and gay men we knew who were proud of their relationships. We wanted to celebrate our commitment to each other in front of family, friends, and colleagues at work and to provide an occasion upon which we could perform a ritual that would involve those who have been supportive of us. We frequently talk with friends about the lack of ritual in lesbian and gay relationships and the positive effects such folkways have on relationships and the creation of community. In applying for RDP status we also welcomed the opportunity to benefit from the same legal rights and obligations that fall to our heterosexual friends and acquaintances.

Not all lesbians and gay men are fortunate enough to have the support and nurturance from those closest to them, and many spoke of this. Barry and Greg, who live in British Columbia and have been together for over eighteen years, have kept their partnership a secret from their families. They have done this not only because of their families' religious beliefs but also because of their fear of public exposure and ridicule:

> We have a small group of friends who we are out to, but other than that no one in either of our families knows about us. Greg is a doctor, and we live in a rural sort of community, which would freak out if they found out about us. Both of our families are very religious, and it would kill my mother if she knew I was gay. She prays for queers all the time in the hopes that God will cure them. If we could we would like to marry, but not while we still live here and not while our parents are alive. I know that we should get wills done and that sort of thing, but neither of us could face our families finding out, which they would if we left each other all our stuff.

Jennie and Chris, who live in rural Nova Scotia and have been together for eleven years, are not out to either their families or their community. They explained that they took a "great risk" in completing the questionnaire, but they wanted to participate in the research because it "made them think about the legal stuff." They also expressed concern that, as they had both been in heterosexual marriages, if they did not make end-of-life decisions, then their ex-husbands might "get everything." As Jennie stated:

> When I saw this questionnaire in *Wayves* it kind of scared me because it made me think that we haven't done anything about any of the will stuff, and if one of us died tomorrow the other wouldn't get a thing. I am sixty-one now and Chris is fifty-eight, and when you get older it makes you wonder. We both have husbands and five kids between us. The kids, well, some of them might know because we just have the one bedroom and stuff and tell them that I sleep on the couch. But we haven't ever told them, and I would hate to think that if I died Chris would have to move out of our house. I own it but we have lived together since the start of her living here, so really half of it should be hers. It's too bad there isn't a place we could go to make a will without everyone knowing your business, but I guess we could get to a lawyer in the city.

Kate and Jill tell a similar story. They, too, live in rural Nova Scotia and are in an eleven-year relationship. Kate explained that they had not registered their relationship because:

> We are not "highly" out because my partner does not wish to have her family "know" — officially. Therefore it is due to fear of being outed inadvertently. Otherwise we don't know how to register with RDP or what the consequences of registering might be. Because my partner is still married we haven't done any wills or medical directives, but we have discussed them over the past ten years. Especially when people in gay relationships have died and their partner is not being credited as such.

Of the women who participated in the research, several said that they were still involved in heterosexual marriages that had not yet been dissolved by divorce. This was the main reason why the couples had not chosen to register their relationships or make end-of-life decisions. Beth, who lives in Nova Scotia and who is in a six-year relationship, said:

> We have not registered our relationship primarily because my partner has not yet divorced her ex-husband. In my opinion, formalizing this partnership — either by registering it as a domestic partnership or having a public commitment ceremony — is highly unethical, and hypocritical, as long as that marriage remains intact.

Aimee, who lives in Nova Scotia and is in a four-year relationship, echoed Beth's views:

> Pam is still married to her ex-husband, and even though he seems supportive of our relationship he is also unwilling to give her a divorce at this time. I think he thinks she will "get over it." She hasn't pushed for a divorce because they have two teenage kids, and we are worried that he would try to stop her from seeing them if she gets too pushy about the divorce thing. They are really old enough to decide for themselves, but we don't want them to have to deal with anything like that until they leave home. It leaves us in a bit of a mess in terms of making end-of-life decisions, I suppose, because legally he is her next of kin. I have been keeping a list of what I own though, so that he doesn't get any of my stuff if I die before she does.

Robin raised many issues that were discussed in the focus groups, particularly by women who have children. First, most of them expressed the fear that ex-husbands would stop them from being seeing their children should they push for a divorce; second, they are concerned about what will happen to their partner, especially with regard to property, when one of them dies. Louise and Joan, who live in Ottawa and who have been together for almost thirteen years, raised this issue:

> We bought the house together but put it in Joan's name because

she was never married and my [Louise's] husband would definitely find out about our relationship if we had bought jointly because he works in the local bank and everyone knows everyone else's business here. I wanted to make a will after I got cancer two years ago but I wasn't sure how to go about leaving the house to Joan and not have everyone wondering how come. My kids are off to university now so they can make up their own minds about whether or not they can accept me, but we haven't told them, and, after all this time of us being together, I can't think how to do that. I hate that they will think we lied to them all these years.

Clearly, the experiences of lesbians who had been (or were still) married were very different from the experiences of those who had not been married. Interestingly, this was not an issue raised by gay men in either the focus groups or in response to the questionnaire.

Even though those who became registered domestic partners saw this as a positive step in their relationships, many also recognized that the legislation in Nova Scotia did not go far enough. As Jim, who is in a ten-year relationship, noted:

The RDP can be dissolved all too easily. We want the same responsibility for our relationship as married couples, we don't want to walk away from them by one of us just popping into the department of vital statistics and filling out a form. Lesbians and gay men put a lot of work and energy into our relationships and we want them to work out.

Jocelyn, who is from Nova Scotia and is in a four-year relationship, agreed with Jim's sentiment:

I think that divorce is too easily available for heterosexual couples and the RDP is too easy to get annulled if you get fed up with each other. We don't take this decision to become legally partnered lightly, and neither should we be able to dissolve those relationships so easily.

In order to dissolve an RDP in Nova Scotia one is merely required to complete a form that can be mailed to the Department of Vital Statistics in Halifax. Clearly, many respondents from this province felt that such an easy exit from the relationship served to trivialize it. Ron, who is in a twelve-year relationship, talked about how difficult it had been for himself and his partner, Les, to tell their families about their relationship when they decided to apply for an RDP. He also felt that it was too easy to become "unregistered."

> We were not sure that we wanted to do the RDP thing; we were worried that our families, [our] parents in particular, would not support us. We were worried about combining our finances in case the relationship fell apart. We really thought it through. When we found out how easy it was to simply fill out a form to end the registration we were frankly shocked. It's like, even though we can do the RDP, it still isn't seen as a legitimate full-time thing. With marriage at least they make you work it out for a year!

The debate around whether or not to register same-sex relationships or to join the ongoing struggle for the legal right to marry was resolved neither in the focus groups nor in the responses to the questionnaire. The majority of respondents, however, agreed that those who wished to so should be supported in legally formalizing their relationship either through RDPs or through marriage. Many saw this right as fundamental and expressed concern that, in North America in general, and in Canada in particular, a public debate was being held as to whether or not lesbians and gay men should have the same rights as heterosexuals.

The issue of same-sex marriage is currently in the news as the Parliamentary Standing Committee on Justice and Human Rights travels across the country to solicit public opinion on this topic. The committee, which is comprised of eighteen Members of Parliament representing the five parties in the House of Commons, is examining the prospect of legalizing same-sex marriage. This committee was struck after the British Columbia Court of Appeal (2003), the Ontario Superior Court (1999), and the Quebec Superior Court (2002) declared that limiting the definition of marriage to heterosexual couples was unconstitutional. The courts gave the government a year to change the law, but it has not been able to decide how to proceed. (See also Chapter 1, Update)

Many gay rights groups and advocates have argued that some of the standing committee members are homophobic and that the hearings are essentially a forum for the opponents of gay marriage to express their views. John Fisher, executive director of EGALE Canada, has claimed that the hearings "could well shape up to be one of the largest gay-bashing exercises in Canadian history. ... We've been called immoral, there's a contempt of gays, of lesbians and the hearings are a farce" (<http://www.egale.ca>, 24 March 24 2003).

On Monday, 7 April 2003, the standing committee held meetings in Halifax, Nova Scotia, at the Halifax Sheraton Hotel. I attended these hearings in order to experience first-hand the tone and substance of the sessions. What follows is a brief account of what transpired.

The meeting was scheduled from 8:30 AM to 5:00 PM, with a one-hour lunch break. The order of the day included six sessions in which presenters were given up to seven minutes to make a presentation (some had previously produced papers that were then read, but this was not always the case), then each committee member was allowed up to three minutes for questions. There were seven committee members present: four representing the Liberal Party of Canada, two representing the Canadian Alliance Party, one representing the Parti Québécois. There were no representatives of either the Progressive Conservative Party or the New Democratic Party. Each session lasted for an hour, and three groups of individuals made presentations to the committee. (This sequence of events was common for all of the hearings held across the country.) Throughout the day there were approximately 120 persons present, including those from the communities at large. People were free to come and go as they pleased throughout the day, and it was common for members of various religious congregations to attend while their clergy members were speaking and then to leave. During the day there were five presentations from members of religious groups, five presentations from individuals not representing any group or organizations, three presentations from members of lesbian and gay organizations, and four presentations from the Gander Status of Women Committee. The Canadian Union of Public Employees of Nova Scotia also made a presentation. In total, eighteen groups and/or individuals made presentations to the committee. Those who spoke in support of granting same-sex couples the right to marry talked of providing equality to all Canadians, granting lesbians and gay men the dignity of marriage, and allowing lesbians and gay men the personal freedom to choose whether or not to marry. Those who spoke against granting lesbians and gay men the right to marry frequently invoked notions of marriage as an event that exists exclusively for heterosexual couples and for the sole purpose of reproduction.

Every member of the clergy who presented suggested that allowing same-sex couples to marry would "open the floodgates to polygamy, bestiality and pedophilia and would threaten the stability of Canadian society" (Reverend Glen Good, Temple Baptist Church). Even though not all clergy members used Good's words, they certainly all invoked the same concepts. Further, they argued that, if the government insisted on legalizing same-sex marriages, and if ministers refused to conduct such services in their churches, then they would be arrested and funds from governments to religious institutions would be diminished or withheld. This blatant attempt at scare-mongering had the desired effect on members of the religious congregations with whom I sat, many of whom were looking at each other and saying, "Shame, shame."

Reverend Lewis H. How, an Anglican minister from the Parish of St. George in Halifax, stated very forcefully that "same-sex relationships are unchristian and furthermore the idea that *justice* and *tolerance* demands the legal acceptance of same-sex 'marriages' is patently false, inflammatory and harmful" (How 2003: n.p., emphasis in original). Nena Sandoval (2003: 2), a clinical sexologist from St. John's, Newfoundland, presented a paper in which she noted that much of the current discrimination against gays and lesbians comes from fundamentalist religious and right-wing political organizations:

> Historically, religious groups have harboured many of the prejudices that exist against gay and lesbian persons not only on the basis of scripture but on erroneous beliefs that homosexuals are somehow a threat to society (e.g., those homosexuals are pedophiles in spite of the empirical research that concludes that the majority of pedophiles are heterosexual).

Brian Boutellier, a member of the congregation of the Safe Harbour Metropolitan Church, located in Halifax, argued in his presentation that "one can be a lesbian or gay man and still love god and be loved by him":

This is an issue of human justice. God loves us as we are. Marriage should be allowed for same-sex couples. I am saddened by the fact that we are here having to fight for our dignity our love for each other, and for god. The dignity of our relationship is paramount. How can we have dignity if the government will not allow us to marry? It is as though we are being told to go to the back of the bus.

My overall reactions to the hearings were of great sadness and fear. Many of the questions to presenters made by committee members were also offensive, especially those made by one Canadian Alliance member, Vic Toews, who said: "Traditional support for churches will be withdrawn if the government requires them to grant same-sex marriages, as well schools might also lose their funding if they refuse to educate students that homosexuality is wrong and immoral." In many cases, rather than ask specific questions, committee members used their three-minute question period to make their own presentations. Interestingly, no female members of the committee were present (there were only two women on the entire eighteen-member committee).

Rather than being a discussion of the legality of including same-sex relationships in the Canadian definition of marriage, the session seemed to be devoted to attacking lesbian and gay lifestyles, questioning the religious and moral authority of our relationships and of us as individuals, and generally creating an "us"-and-"them" reality for the Canadian population.

The session raised issues relating to the effectiveness of lesbian/gay parenting; of educating children; of allowing and welcoming us into churches, synagogues, and mosques; and even of the ability of people of the same sex to love one another. Especially troubling to me were the links drawn between two people of the same-sex loving each other and "bestiality, polygamy and pedophilia." The Web site Equal Marriage (<http://www.samesexmarriage.ca/>) has been covering the hearings on a daily basis and providing an overview of what has transpired. On 26 March 2003 it printed a summary of some of the comments made thus far. These include:

Witnesses appearing before the parliament's Standing Committee on Justice and Human Rights have said that homosexuals:

- Are an "aberration" that will cause the "destruction of our civilization." (Feb. 6)
- Would "create a new morality in which homosexuality is not merely tolerated but is normalized and would branch out into sexual activity with babies, children of both sexes, and with animals." (Feb. 11)
- Are comparable to alcoholics. (Feb. 11)
- Become gay because of childhood molestations. (Feb. 11)
- Are mostly drug users, unlike heterosexuals. (Feb. 12)
- Can change sexual orientation: "It seems it's acquired." (Feb. 12)
- Are more prone to infidelity than heterosexuals. (Feb. 12)
- Could be induced to "abstain or leave the country if body parts are lopped off." (Feb. 13)
- Have gained rights in cases "based on emotionalism, the quivering lip and teary eye" but "thank God, [rights for gays] can be repealed." (Feb. 13)
- Are "repugnant" and "detestable" and when gays have been tolerated in society, "God providentially and in judgment wiped those civilizations off the face of the earth." (Feb. 18).
- All of the above statements went unchallenged by Andy Scott (Liberal Party), the chair of the committee. He seems to have given a free pass to certain guests of the committee who spew hateful comments about gays. (Extended Run For Cruel Joke: Committee Seems a Mockery of Justice)

At the committee hearing in Toronto on 12 April 2003, Wayne Samuelson, the head of the Ontario Federation of Labour, accused the committee of doing nothing to stop the "insulting, dangerous and unnecessary" rhetoric coming from conservative Christian groups opposed to gay marriage. He also blasted the committee after speakers from groups opposed to gay marriage stated that homosexuality is linked to pedophilia, bestiality, and mental illness:

> I have three daughters and one is gay. I'm insulted to hear these suggestions that my daughter must suffer from STDs or binge

drinking because she is gay — give me a break. In all my years of public policy discussion I have never seen these kinds of incredibly destructive comments allowed. (Cited in Sui 2003c)

It is not difficult to understand the fear of right-wing Christian groups and others who are threatened by a change in the status quo — a change that would open up the institution of marriage to same-sex partners. Lost would be the great advantages of heterosexual privilege, of power and control over women and children, and the entire illusion of normalcy that such groups presently and exclusively enjoy. It is more difficult to understand why elected politicians would allow a theoretically public forum to be used as a site for a blatant display of the acceptance and reinforcement of homophobia — unless they fear the power of the religious right when it comes to re-election.

The hearings are scheduled to wind down later in the spring, and a report to Parliament is expected to be handed down in the fall. It will be interesting to see whether or not the Canadian government is prepared to grant equal marriage rights to all of its citizens, in spite of this resulting in what many say will be the overthrow of society!

O'Brien and Weir (1995: 132) in an article addressing lesbians and gay men both inside and outside families, note that we are consistently portrayed in politics, the media, the law, and the educational and child welfare systems as

> menacing "the family." When legislation that might benefit lesbians and gay men is debated, the legal changes are cast as an attack on families. We see here evidence of a pervasive ideology that holds that gay men and lesbians are outside of and detrimental to families. This homophobic and heterosexist ideology has been firmly implanted in the Canadian state and is found everywhere, from hospital insurance plans to child adoptions to social benefits.

Such concerns for the "family" are unnecessary for several reasons, the family being an institution that has changed drastically over the years in response to industrialization, the increased equality of the roles between women and men (and adults and children), the high divorce rate in Canada (and the resulting increase of blended and single-parent families), and so on. In any case, the notion that the parenting abilities of same-sex couples are somehow different from those of heterosexual couples, or that these couples are threatening to the stability of the family, has not been supported by research. In a paper produced for the Vanier Institute of the Family in 2003, sociologist Dr. Ann-Marie Ambert offered an extensive review of the literature and research available on same-sex couples and the families that they create and from which they originate. While acknowledging that very little research has been conducted in this area, Ambert points out that the existing data are inconclusive and that, in general, there would appear to be no differences between how heterosexuals parent and how lesbians and gay men parent, in the sexual preferences of their children, with regard to levels of domestic violence, in the psychological adjustment of their children, and so on (Ambert 2003).

Those who argue that the Canadian family will be in jeopardy if same-sex partners are able to marry or have children do not recognize that a great number of lesbians and gay men are already parents from previous heterosexual relationships, that the children raised in those families are as well adjusted as are those who have been brought up in heterosexual unions, and that the Canadian family, like all social institutions, is constantly changing.

If lesbians and gay men were allowed to marry, or otherwise register their relationships so that, in law, they were considered to be "spouses," then their end-of-life decisions would be placed on an equal footing with those of heterosexual couples. In other words, partners would be legally listed as next-of-kin with regard to medical, pension, funeral/cremation, and other related decisions. These are the sorts of "rights" that those who support marriage for same-sex partners wish to obtain. They also want to see our relationships recognized in every province and territory in Canada rather than just in Nova Scotia, Manitoba, Quebec, and, as of June 2003, Ontario.

Chapter Five

End-of-Life Decisions Made by Lesbians and Gay Men

I said earlier that the majority of respondents had made end-of-life decisions. More men than women felt that this was "a crucial and necessary component of living together (Karl, Alberta, in a seven-year relationship with Bob). Most respondents had completed wills, living wills, medical directives, and had appointed partners as legal powers of attorney. Taking out life insurance policies was not common among respondents, and some noted that they had such services available as part of an employment package. Three men noted that they were unable to designate their partners as beneficiaries to their life insurance policies because their companies did not cover same-sex partners. According to Nick, who is from Scarborough and is in a fourteen-year relationship:

> When we went to get life insurance we were told that we couldn't have each other as designated beneficiaries because they don't recognize that as legitimate in law. We were together for eight years then so Barry stayed with that company, but I changed mine to one at work. If this happened to us today we would take the insurance people to court. We have human rights now, sort of!

Approximately 67 percent of informants said that they had joint bank accounts, even though many noted that they also retained separate accounts for their sole use. Danny and John, who are from Ontario and have been together for four years, said: "We have joint accounts where we handle all of the condo bills, mortgage, repairs, household stuff, meals and travel. But we also keep our own accounts for personal use so that we don't get into control issues about money and who can buy what when." Those who said that they did not have joint accounts also expressed the idea that these put unnecessary pressure on the relationship. According to

Len and Dick, who are from Ontario and are in a three-year relationship: "We don't feel any need to have joint bank accounts. We divide every-thing down the middle and that isn't a problem for either of us. I think having joint accounts is too restrictive and too much like a marriage. Why put unnecessary pressures on the relationship." Carla and Denise, who live in Nova Scotia and who have been in a relationship for six years, adopt another point of view: "For us, getting joint bank accounts was an imperative. It was like saying, 'I am willing to share my financial re-sources with you. I am committed to the relationship even in monetary terms.' Really we supported the idea that 'what's yours is mine' and vice versa."

Approximately 40 percent of respondents stated that they had taken measures to ensure joint ownership of property, either by buying homes together or, if one partner owned a home prior to the relationship, taking out joint tenancy on the property or having the non-owner buy out half of the mortgage or lease. As well as full-time residential properties, some informants said that they also jointly purchased cottages and other forms of recreational property. In response to this question respondents also mentioned that they jointly owned automobiles, recreation vehicles, land, and an assortment of household appliances as well as animals and farm vehicles.

It was more common for those who had completed RDP applications to acquire the aforementioned legal documents than it was for those who had not done so. The completion of legal arrangements was seen as an important component of the planning for such events. Normally, when completing a legal will most individuals also completed a living will or medical directive and appointed their partner as health guardian (or the provincial equivalent). As well, most said that they had given their partner legal power of attorney. Some of the reasons for acquiring the legal documents described above were provided by Dee and Denise, who live in Nova Scotia and have been together for almost two years:

> We had estate-planning sessions and so we both had legal rights with respect to one another. My previous will had a relative as executor but now that Dee is in my life I wanted her to get everything. Dee has a condo, RRSP, and a pension plan; but I had no other assets so I went and got life insurance to fill the void in case

something happened to me. We plan to get joint bank accounts and make the condo jointly owned too.

George and Ross, also from Nova Scotia and in a fourteen-year relationship, stressed the importance of making a legal will and appointing a health guardian. This was brought home to them through their experiences with friends who had died of AIDS:

> We felt it extremely important to make our relationship legal and valid and to avoid any influence from our families. We have seen so many of our friends left with nothing when their partners died, usually of AIDS. We wanted to avoid that scenario so we were very careful about getting the appropriate documents signed. Really, doing these things is like putting icing on the cake, it just makes everything so much clearer. We also completed a sort of prenuptial arrangement before we started living together to ensure that if we ever broke up, each would get the equivalent of what he put into the relationship at the beginning. Really, for a lot of families, being able to swoop down and take everything out of the home after the partner dies is a sort of act of final revenge for the surviving partner "corrupting" their child.

Whereas many male participants discussed the need for the equivalent of prenuptial arrangements, none of the females did so. Vicky and Barb, who live in Nova Scotia and who have been together for over twenty years, said in a focus group meeting that, in their experiences in the lesbian and gay community, men are more likely to be "business-like" and "organized" than are women. Vicky noted that:

> When we first got together our best friends, Norm and Brian, insisted that we have some sort of prenuptial arrangement, even though we had already lived together for two years then. It seemed a bit late to us. But they kept telling us, "if you do all this legal stuff don't you want to ensure that you get out of the relationship what you put into it should you split up?" It all seemed very business-like to us, but I know that in the gay male community this is very much expected when two guys move in together.

George and Matt, who were in the same focus group as were Vicky and Barb, and who have been together for nineteen years, agreed that gay men are more likely than are lesbians to be careful about securing the assets they bring into relationships. George felt that this was so because men, regardless of sexual preference, are socialized to "be careful with their money and possessions." He further noted:

> I think that lesbians are too trusting really, and there are all those jokes about what do two lesbians do after they have been seeing [sic] each other twice — they rent a U-Haul and move in together. [He laughs] Having seen so many relationships in the gay male community end in acrimonious ways it makes sense to me to ensure that, when a relationship ends, no one is getting screwed and losing some of their stuff. It is just the sensible thing to do.

Lionel and Tom have been together for eight years. Lionel is a lawyer, originally from Montreal and now living in Nova Scotia. He stressed the need for lesbians and gay men to make end-of-life decisions and to be out in order to, as he put it, "make them stick." He spoke of the many clients he has had over the years who had made legal end-of-life decisions in which their partners were the beneficiaries of wills and estates but who had not informed their families and heterosexual friends of their relationships.

> I had these very sweet old guys who had been together for about thirty years. One of them owned the house his mother had left him and he just assumed that, because he made Bill his beneficiary in his will, that everything would be fine. Had I been his original lawyer I would have told him this wouldn't necessarily work. Anyway, when he died his sister tried to get the house, and she insisted that Bill was just an old friend who lived with Jim and who had no entitlement to the house, which was quite valuable. She contested the will and everything, had the expensive lawyer looking into it, and Bill almost lost everything he had put into their home. Fortunately we were able to show that Jim's intentions were to have Bill stay in the house and we had to get witnesses to say that they were a couple and everything. So not only did Bill have to go

to court to get what was legally his, he also had to be outed and Jim's family had to hear, after he died, that he had been a homosexual for all of his life. What a terrible way for people to have to deal with their grief.

When asked why they had obtained legal wills and the other documents and policies, most informants said that they wanted to ensure that their partners were not left, as Joan from British Columbia said, "in the middle of the lake without a paddle." As well, several respondents expressed the concern that ex-partners or children might contest any arrangements made if a partner should die. Lynn, who is from British Columbia and is in a five-year relationship with Joan, said:

> Joan's ex is a lawyer, and when they split up she was really furious and tried to get the house away from her and everything. She even took the dogs and the garden furniture when Joan was at work. Anyway, it was a real mess. They were together for almost sixteen years and there were all sorts of legal hassles. We made a pre-relationship agreement so that if either of us died the other would get everything, the same as if we split up. Mostly we were concerned that her ex would claim that everything that was Joan's was now hers, no matter how long we were together. We made it all legal and everything, and our lawyer has a copy and so do we.

Kim and Stacey also live in British Columbia, and they have been together for eighteen years. Kim was previously married and has two teenage children who are not supportive of their mother's relationship with Stacey or of her sexual preference. Indeed, Stacey noted that the youngest child, a daughter, is "sickened by the thought of her Mum being a lesbian." She went on:

> We went the whole ten yards when we took out wills, living wills, insurance policies, medical stuff — the works. Her youngest kid hates us both now that her mum is out, and we know that if anything ever happened to her when Liz is older that she would try to get everything from me. Her son is not so bad, but who knows

who he might get involved with down the road, and they might try to get him to get everything. It's scary really and such a great big piss off that you have to worry about your own kids ripping you off.

Most who responded to this part of the questionnaire spoke of the need to ensure such things as an "equal partnership and protection from family influence" (Ryan, Nova Scotia, in a ten-year relationship). According to Kellie, who lives in Nova Scotia and is in a seven-year relationship, "I was interested in ensuring that my wishes were known and put in place regarding all of the above. A will, power of attorney, living will, and medical directive allowed me to do that and to ensure that what I wanted to occur is likely to occur." According to Jill and Heather, who live in Nova Scotia and who have been in a same-sex relationship for the past six years, "We got most of these to protect each other's ownership — haven't obtained the others yet as we have both come out of previous relationships and are undoing those." Lisa and Bev, who live in Ontario and who have been in a relationship for six and a half years, summed up the feelings of many when they said:

> It is important for all families and individuals to make proper legal arrangements, especially for same-sex couples. In the past, families and courts have not recognized same-sex relationships. We did not want our wishes or our relationship ignored upon death and feel it is vital to have all matters taken care of well in advance. It is our responsibility to ensure our legal rights are respected.

In general, the responses to this part of the questionnaire invoked notions of wanting to support and protect relationships and the individuals within them, to provide partners with legal protection in times of illness and death, and to indicate "our love, respect and importance to one another always, but especially in times of crisis" (Bob, Nova Scotia, in a ten-year relationship).

A small minority (8 percent) of female respondents stated that they either already had or were planning to have children. These women saw it as imperative that legal arrangements be made to safeguard their partner's joint guardianship of children, assets, and property.

When asked if, as a couple, they had discussed a variety of end-of-life issues, responses varied. I now present them in the order the topics were listed in the questionnaire:

Medical Treatment Decisions

The vast majority of informants said that they had had discussions about medical treatment decisions. This was especially so in the focus groups in Nova Scotia, where some rural respondents expressed concern that not all medical treatments were available in local hospitals, with the result that transportation and time off work would be issues for both the person with an illness and her/his partner. As Joanne and Barb, who live in rural Nova Scotia and are in a nine-year relationship, noted:

> Well, since Barb's Mum got sick with cancer we have really needed to talk about this. She needs some special type of radiation that you can only get in the city, and so someone has to travel there with her three times a week. It really made us think about what will happen if either of us has to go through that. We even talk about moving to the city to be nearer the hospital there, especially if it is true that cancer is passed down through the generations, especially to the women in the family.

June and Benita have been together for more than eight years and used to live in a small rural town in Nova Scotia. When June's multiple sclerosis forced her into a wheelchair and her many medical needs became evident, they decided to move to the city where help was more readily available. According to Benita:

> We had to move to Halifax as soon as the MS got worse, we didn't really have much choice and we had talked about this for a long time. We had hoped that these sorts of medical decisions would be easier to make, but they were a real challenge for us. It was hard to find an apartment in the city that was wheelchair accessible, and June has to have someone come in every day to help with personal care. These aren't things you want to talk about in a relationship, but you had better because you never know when one of you might need medical care.

Generally, couples recognized the need to discuss medical treatment decisions, although few mentioned any health problems that would cause this discussion to take on a more imminently serious tone.

Funeral/Burial/Cremation Wishes

The majority of respondents said that they had had discussions regarding funerals/cremations/burials, although some noted that they had not because they simply did not want to talk about "such depressing topics." For example, Gina, who lives in Alberta and is in a four-year relationship, commented: "I am really scared to die so I don't go there in terms of this stuff. I mean life is for the living so who wants to talk about death. I would find that really depressing and sad."

Jake, who is from Ontario and is in a one-year relationship, had a different attitude:

> My last partner died of AIDS and we never talked about this sort of thing. When he died I had no idea whether he wanted to be buried or cremated or any of that. He was from the Philippines and his parents didn't know he was gay and we had never met. So I had to make all of the funeral arrangements, and I tell you I was pretty freaked out about whether I was doing what he wanted or not. He was a very shy sort of guy and even his friends didn't know. We were together for eleven years and never once talked about this sort of thing. I wonder how that can be, that we know so little about each other.

Many noted that their discussions about funeral and burial preferences were precipitated by the deaths of friends, ex-lovers, and family members. As Beth, who lives in Nova Scotia and who is in a six-year relationship, stated:

> Many of our conversations about these issues have been prompted by the death of a close friend or someone in our circle of friends or relatives. When I was partnered with Meredith, her chronic illness and the possibility of a recurrence of breast cancer prompted us to have a medical power of attorney drawn up so that if anything happened I could make all the necessary decisions. We wanted to

make sure that the decisions I made about her [having a] celebration of life rather than a funeral would be in keeping with the choices we had made together rather than the choices I would make for her. When M and I started becoming partners six years ago, we talked about the types of things we might need in order to ensure that we would be comfortable making these choices together. So far we both prefer to be cremated, and this is important because her kids need to know that too, as well as her ex-husband.

Many male respondents provided me with stories about the deaths of friends and acquaintances through HIV/AIDS and related illnesses. They spoke of how these particular deaths impressed upon them the importance of making one's wishes about final disposition known. Jim, who is from Nova Scotia and is in a nine-year relationship, related the following:

> One of our best friends, Jake, was sick with AIDS for about six years. He had been in a relationship for about six years with Rod, but prior to that he had been married with two teenage sons. He had all kinds of guilt and other issues around that, so he was never willing to discuss any of his final wishes. I suppose he didn't want to have a fight between his ex-wife and kids and Rod. He just couldn't come to terms with it all before he died. So when he did die, in a great deal of pain and in a confused and anxious state, it was left to Rod to try to figure our what he would have wanted. His ex-wife was really cut up about it, and she wanted him buried near where he used to live in Middleton. But Rod wanted him cremated and scattered in Scott's Bay because they hiked there in the summer. It was a total mess and we didn't want anything like that going on for either of us.

Bob, who lives in Ontario and who is in a four-year relationship, spoke about his partner, Luke's, friend, who also died of AIDS:

> Luke had this friend [Warren] in the military who had AIDS and died from it two years ago. They were not at all out and never discussed anything at all about the end of their days together. When it was obvious that Luke was going to die, his lover did try to get him to

say what he wanted in terms of funeral arrangements; but he was too scared to die and so never discussed it with him. If he had it would have been so much easier for everyone in the community, but especially for his lover.

In both the focus groups and in the responses to the questionnaire, many men spoke of experiences similar to those related by Jim and Bob. In doing so they reiterated the need for couples to make end-of-life decisions and to live in a country where their relationships are a source of pride rather than of fear. They also spoke of a need for end-of-life education, information, and resources that are aimed at same-sex as well as at opposite-sex partners.

Even though the majority of respondents said that they did discuss decisions relating to medical treatment and final dispositions, fewer talked about the various options and services available. This may simply have been because informants were not familiar with what was available in their communities, or it may have been because they were not willing to discuss where they wanted to die. Lisa, who is from Nova Scotia and who is in a seven-year relationship with Jan, put it this way:

> First of all I doubt that most people know where they want to die or what might be involved. I know from what Jan [who is a nurse] says that dying at home isn't always that easy to do, especially if you can't afford the special care nurses. We don't discuss this aspect of our lives at all. It gives me the creeps to talk about death, and Jan sees too much of it in her job.

Mike, a paramedic who lives in Toronto and is in an eleven-year relationship, sees things rather differently:

> I see death a lot in my work. I think it is really important to talk to your partner about where you want to die, but you both have to be comfortable with it. I think being with someone who is dying is a gift, but then I am trained to be able to do that kind of work. I would be happy to be with Barry, and he with me, in our own home when the time comes. I know this isn't true for lots of gay men.

Again, as with funeral, cremation, and burial wishes, many spoke of their past experiences concerning the deaths of friends, family, and others with whom they were familiar. Jason, who lives in Alberta and is in a one-year relationship with Win, talked about a friend who died last year:

> When Jack got sick no one knew how to take care of him or what was to come. He wanted to die at home, but his partner was scared of what might happen. He had lung cancer and was coughing all the time and being out of breath, it hurt just to listen to him trying to breathe. Lots of us agreed to assist in caring for him to die at home, but no one had the money to take time off work. So he had to go to the hospital, which he really hated, especially being gay and all. It really bothered us all because we wanted him to be happy in death. He wasn't, and he died in the hospital. When Win and me got together we had all of this out because we had both known Jack, and neither of us wanted to go like that. We want to die at home, and we are going to get the long-term care insurance as soon as it comes out to make that happen when the time comes.

Carrie, who lives in Nova Scotia and who is in an eight-year relationship, spoke about the death of her friend's partner:

> When we had been together about seven years our good friend's partner died. They had been very closeted for all of their relationship in terms of their families, but when she was dying our friend decided to come out to her mother. She thought it would make things easier on her partner if everything was out in the open. Instead of that, her mother would not let her partner in the hospital room and she had to sneak in when the mother was out getting stuff. It was a truly gross situation because Alma had wanted to die at home but then she couldn't because her mother wouldn't accept Rosie taking care of her. So she died in the hospital in the end, and Rosie wasn't there at the time, and she got the call at work.

Many spoke of their need to come out of the closet in order to have these discussions not only with each other but also with family members and so avoid exactly the sort of situation that Carrie described.

Some people, especially those who attended churches that were affiliated with particular care facilities, invoked the notion of religious belief when speaking about where they wanted to die. Dee, who lives in Cape Breton and who is in a thirteen-year relationship, spoke about her Roman Catholicism and her desire to die in the same hospital as her parents.

> I was raised Roman Catholic and my family has always lived in Cape Breton. We were all born in the same Straight Regional Hospital, and every one of my family [members] has died there too. The priest visits there all the time too, so we didn't really discuss where I wanted to die, I just said that when the time comes I want to die in the hospital like the rest of my family. For me it's a sort of "roots" and tradition thing.

Terry, who is a Huron from Ontario and who is in a twenty-year relationship with Rick, had a different view of tradition:

> In my culture, which is Aboriginal, we prefer to die at home with our family. Even though Rick is White he agrees that I should be able to go home when the time comes. I am not religious, but I prefer the Aboriginal ways of dealing with dying people [to] the White-man's ways. We have lots of drumming and dancing and connecting with the great spirit. That is so much better than lying in a quiet hospital bed. Now if Rick goes first, I don't know what we'll do [laughs]!

Organ Donations

When I formulated the questions for the questionnaire, I included one about organ donations without realizing that, in Canada and elsewhere, gay men are prohibited from donating blood, blood products, tissues, cells, or organs even if they are HIV negative. Among the focus-group men with whom I spoke, and in responses to the questionnaire as well as in chat rooms, this topic was a highly sensitive one. There were a number of reasons for this, most of which have to do with the obvious discriminatory practices of the Canadian blood supply agency and the various provincial transplant policies.

According to the Canadian Blood Services Agency "male donors who have had sex with other males, or female donors who have had sex with males who have had sex with other males" are ineligible to donate blood or blood products. This is due to the agency's attempt to "reduce the risk of HIV transmission" (Lisa Bussell, Communications Officer, personal e-mail communication, 19 February 2003). Even though a homosexual man's HIV test may be negative, and even if he has had only one partner, he is still ineligible to donate blood.

Even though gay men recognized that blood agencies need to carefully screen potential donors and to reject those who may be involved in behaviour that poses a risk to others, many nonetheless also expressed the opinion that a blanket refusal to accept the blood of gay men was discriminatory. George, who is a volunteer firefighter living in Ontario and is in a seventeen-year relationship, expressed his surprise when he went to donate blood and found that, based on his responses to the agency's questionnaire, he would not be allowed to do so.

> I was asked to fill out a donor questionnaire and it asked stuff about "have you had sex with a man since 1977." I put "yes," and the woman told me that I couldn't give blood because of that. I told her that me and Don had been together since we were in high school, that neither of us had had other lovers, that I would have as many AIDS tests as they wanted, but she said that they could not take my blood. Now they had had this huge plea for blood, and it just seemed like they were discriminating against us because we were gay men.

Barry, who is from Nova Scotia and is in a twelve-year relationship, also attempted to donate blood and was refused due to his acknowledged homosexuality. He explained it this way:

> I work at the hospital and they are always having these blood drives, so I went along to give some of mine. I was asked to fill out a long form, and I asked the woman about it. I did tell her that I was a gay man and that I was in a long-term relationship with Rick, and that when we first got together we both had HIV tests because that was something we wanted to be sure about. She said because of that

I couldn't donate blood, even though I tested negative. I tried to take it up with my supervisor and he called the Canadian Blood Services people because he agreed that it was discrimination, but they wouldn't budge. It's just another example of the ways in which we are always being discriminated against, and while I see the need for the blood services people to be careful, and I wouldn't give blood if I was sick with anything, I still think they ought to make exceptions for those of us who test negative to the virus. If Rick or me ever get sick I would want us to be able to give each other blood, but there's no way around it.

The thirty-item questionnaire administered to potential blood donors can be viewed at <http://www.bloodservices.ca>.

According to the regulations of the Canadian General Standards on the Safety of Cells, Tissues and Organs intended for Transplantation and Assisted Reproduction, when assessing potential organ/tissue or cell donors males are given a questionnaire that contains the question: "Have you had sex with a man who in the past five years had sex with another man?" A positive response to this question will "rule out the donor from donating tissues (e.g., heart valves, bone, and eyes). The donor's organs (e.g., kidney, liver, lungs) may be used for transplantation under exceptional release" (Anita Mahadeo, Regulatory Associate, Health Products and Food Branch, Biologic and Genetic Therapies Directorate, personal e-mail communication, 26 February 2003).

In an attempt to discover what conditions might indicate "exceptional release," I contacted the Nova Scotia Tissue and Organ Transplant Directory and was informed that the exclusionary criteria are mandated under the Canadian Standards for the Safety of Cell, Tissues and Organs, that they clearly state that exclusions include "men who have had sex with another man within the preceding 5 years," and that organs/tissues/cells were never extracted from those who fell into this category (Kate Hackett, Tissue Specialist, Nova Scotia Department of Health, personal e-mail communication, 21 February 2003).

I also contacted the Canadian Standards Association to inquire as to whether or not there have been exceptions made in other provinces with regard to allowing gay men to donate tissues, cells, and organs. I was advised once again that it was extremely unlikely that men who have had sex with men over the past five years would ever be eligible to donate (Nancy Bestic, Project Manager, Health Canada Technology Program, Canadian Standards Association, e-mail communication, 6 February 2003).

What might be the consequences of such legislation and the obvious discrimination against gay men who are willing to have HIV tests to show that they do not carry the virus, or to men who have been in long-term, monogamous relationships with one partner? George, who lives in Nova Scotia and is in an eighteen-year relationship, described the following situation:

> You know, of course, that we are not permitted to donate organs or blood or anything like that. A year ago my niece, Kelly, was diagnosed with some form of hepatitis and was having serious kidney problems, so they put her on a transplant list for a new organ. My sister and her husband were not a match, and they asked me if I would be willing to consider donating a kidney if I could. Nelson and me discussed it and of course we agreed that I would. I talked with my family doctor about it, and he said that I could certainly go and get the tests to see if I were a match. There was no problem with my doing that, I wasn't asked to sign anything at that time that asked about my sexual habits. The tests came back positive and we were all so excited that I could help. Everything was going along fine, and then a nurse at the transplant unit realized that I hadn't filled in any of the forms. Of course I wasn't going to lie about having had sex with my life-partner, and then she told me that I was not eligible because of that. I couldn't believe it. I offered to have an HIV test and I got my doctor to write a letter saying that my health was excellent, which he did. But nothing we did worked. Meanwhile Kelly was getting worse and here I had what could help her. I am not saying that I wasn't scared to give up one of my kidneys mind you, but I had what she needed. We even went to a lawyer to argue that it was discrimination, but he said that that wouldn't work because the rules are so clear. I am so saddened as I watch Kelly's condition get worse and it makes me so mad sometimes that they won't make any exceptions to their stupid rules.

Although I did not hear many stories like this, it does point out the unwillingness on the part of health care professionals to pursue exceptions to the rules when someone's life lies in the balance. As well, such behaviour also indicates the not-so-subtle discrimination against gay men who are more than willing to take any test to prove their assertion that they are not HIV positive. Frank, who is from Ontario and is in an eleven-year relationship, provided the following story of his attempt to donate a kidney to his ex-wife:

> Jen, my ex-wife, was diagnosed with some form of lupus and she was on dialysis at the time. She was on the transplant list but was getting weaker, and we were all pretty worried about her. When Josh, our grandson, was born I talked to Jim about maybe finding out if I were a suitable match so that I could donate one of my kidneys. I had no idea then that they wouldn't take organs from us. Anyway, I spoke with my doctor about it and she was all for it. She did tell me then though that the hospital might not even consider it, seeing as I was a gay man. I met with this specialist guy who told me that even if I was a match they couldn't accept one of my kidney's because of my "lifestyle." I almost wanted to thump him. "This isn't a 'lifestyle,'" I said, "this *is* my life, and Jen is my ex-wife who I care about very much." Anyway, no matter what arguments I used they wouldn't even do the tests to see if I was a match. I offered to do everything and anything they wanted to make sure that I didn't have AIDS, but nothing worked. It was a case of 100 percent discrimination against me because I am gay. No doubt about it.

Last year a friend who is a lesbian was in a similar situation to Frank's: her ex-husband needed a kidney transplant and, when other family members were tested and found not to be a match, she agreed to be tested. She was found to be compatible and was able to donate a kidney to her ex-husband without suffering any discrimination on the basis of her sexual preference. In their response to the questionnaire many gay men indicated that they had discussed the topic of organ donations, leading me to conclude that perhaps they are unaware of the fact that they are not eligible to do so. If this is the case, then their end-of-life wishes, should they choose to donate organs, would not be realized, and this could have negative emotional and psychological consequences for their partners.

Whereas gay men were particularly concerned about the topic of organ donations, lesbians were not. However, especially in the focus groups, many women expressed their dismay that gay men could not donate blood, organs, or tissues. Jackie, who lives in Nova Scotia and who is in a four-year relationship, said: "Not allowing gay men to donate organs or blood products is the ultimate in discrimination on the grounds of sexuality as far as I am concerned. I am surprised that no one is fighting this situation. It is blatant homophobia."

A small majority of lesbians who participated in the research (57 percent) had made arrangements for organ donations. Sara, who lives in Ontario and who is in a two-year relationship, noted that her partner, Leigh, is in the military, where there is some expectation that organ donor cards will be completed: "We weren't going to fill out the organ donor cards on our driving licences. Just didn't feel comfortable doing that. But Leigh is in the army, and they sort of require you to do that there — sort of like your community responsibility and all that. So we both signed the organ donor forms." By and large, lesbians were more concerned with other types of end-of-life decisions.

Estate Planning and Investments

The majority of respondents who have been in relationships for more than a year noted that they had engaged in estate planning and investment activities, either through taking workshops provided through their places of employment, through personal initiatives, or through sessions offered by various gay and lesbian organizations. Jill, who is from Nova Scotia and is in a three-year relationship, commented:

> We decided to take a course together on estate planning, which included investment opportunities, because we have heard so many stories in the community about lesbians getting dragged through the courts when one became ill or died because they didn't make proper plans. As well, we recognized that, due to our work patterns, our pensions wouldn't be equal, and we wanted to deal with all of this. Especially after we bought the house together.

Lisa, who is also from Nova Scotia and who is in an eight-year relationship, had experienced the death of a close friend who had not made a will or engaged in estate planning. She determined when she and Joanne first got together that they would attend to these matters.

> After we had been together for two years we decided to buy the condo, and right there and then we said let's go and get some advice about estate planning to make sure that, if anything happens to either of us, we shall know that our money is properly invested to take care of the remaining partner and that our home is well protected in terms of the mortgage payments. So we went to this woman who handles both of these, and we now have a greater sense of security if anything happens to either or both of us. When my friend Deb died her family swooped down like vultures to get everything they could from her partner. Because they had not dealt with any of this there was nothing that Bette could do. It was so sad.

Todd and Mike, who are from Ontario and are in an eleven-year relationship, said that they wanted to make their relationship public and decided to so by attending estate-planning and investment-counselling programs put on by one of the local banks. They said:

> We were convinced that we wanted to be public and intentional about our relationship, so when the Royal Bank sent around a notice telling us about these free workshops we decided to go. It was really neat because on the first night we were the only gays there, but at the second session we met these two other guys and we've been good friends ever since. I think that the banks have finally figured out that gays and lesbians buy houses and have money too, so now they want to woo us as well as the straights.

More older lesbians and gay men had discussed the issues of estate planning and investments than had younger ones. For example, Tina, who is from New Brunswick and is in a two-year relationship, commented:

Well, I am only twenty-five and Jeannie is thirty-two; we've only been together for two years and we haven't bought anything together yet. I am sure that, as we stay together longer and get more settled in terms of where we end up living, that we would buy something together and then we would do this.

As well as the fact that younger people may have few or no assets that require the need for estate planning or investments, it was recognized that not all partners in a relationship have equal access to financial resources and that, in these cases, such planning would be inappropriate and might, indeed, raise other issues within the relationship. Pat, who is from Nova Scotia and is in a seven-year relationship, said:

> My partner is the executor of my will, so she will end up having to deal with all of the estate-planning and investment details if I died. At some point we will probably talk about financial planning but I just do the basics with my investments. I haven't done that much financial planning about life either. My partner doesn't have a lot of assets, very few in fact, so it wouldn't be much of an issue.

Tom, who is from Ontario and is in a three-year relationship, noted that the issue of estate planning and financial investments was one that, when first discussed, caused some disagreement between him and his partner, Paul. This topic was first broached after they "passed a graveyard" and then "pondered their immortality":

> Well, I earn a great deal more than Paul, so when I broached the subject of estate planning and such he got really pissed off because he doesn't have any money or those sorts of assets. I own the house and he pays rent. I don't care if he leaves me nothing, but the whole topic of money and assets can be very contentious between us. I am sure that when he gets promoted some of that will change, and I would be happy for him to eventually buy half of the house, or sell it and buy one together that we both own. Even though these topics are really about what happens after death, they are also about how we live our lives. It isn't as though we are here forever, after all, we are just passing through.

Tina lives in British Columbia and is in a sixteen-and-a-half-year relationship. She said that, due to recent illnesses and a serious car accident, she and her partner saw the need to make decisions about estate plans and investments to ensure that, if either of them were incapacitated or worse, the other would be taken care of:

> After we had been together for about six years I had a series of major illnesses, I also had a car accident. Then, after that, Joy also got really sick, so we decided it was time to look into these things to make sure that we were each taken care of if necessary. It really is never too soon to begin these discussions, and I worry that it took us so long to figure it out. But we did it, that's the main thing and now we have one less thing to worry about. Because we are both right now in poorer health, we don't want to obsess about our mortality and what we should have done to make sure that the other is well taken care of.

The topic of estate planning and investments for lesbians and gay men has recently been promoted by several financial planning institutions that have recognized that some members of the lesbian and gay community have well-paying jobs along with other financial and real-estate resources. In Nova Scotia a Halifax-based financial planning company — Boyne, Clarke — has been offering free workshops to the lesbian/gay community. Further to this, articles profiling lesbian and gay couples and their investment strategies have also appeared in the *Globe and Mail* and in such business-oriented magazines as *Report on Business*, *Atlantic Business Monthly*, *The Economist*, and *Business Week*.

Appointing Partners as Legal Guardians of Children

The majority of respondents said that this question was not applicable to their lives either because they did not have children, because their children were now adults, or that the children's biological father would perform this role. Some said that they would prefer that their same-sex partner be appointed legal guardian of their children, and they had made these wishes known in their will. However, they also recognized that, in law, the other legal parent would be appointed as guardian. Consider Carla, who is from Nova Scotia and is in a ten-year relationship:

> Jen and I have been together for nine years now and the kids are fifteen and thirteen. As far as they are concerned she is their other parent. I am divorced, but even so my ex-husband would be given custody of the kids if anything happened to me. I did discuss this with my lawyer, and she said that all I could do was to make my wishes known in my will and request that the kids have a say in where they go to live. They already say that would choose to live with Jen, and, as they get older, they will hopefully be given this choice if I were to die.

Respondents who did have children — from previous heterosexual relationships, through artificial insemination either by anonymous donor or friend, or through adoption — all stated that they had engaged in discussions regarding appointing their partners as legal guardians. This was especially the case for those who had infants, and this applied more often to lesbians than to gay men. Anne, who lives in Nova Scotia and is in a fourteen-and-a-half-year relationship, noted that, when their baby was born some two years ago, both she and her partner made legal provisions to ensure that they would both be registered as parents.

> I was not the birth mother, but I made arrangements to adopt the baby so that we would both be seen as her legal parents in the event that anything happened to May. There wouldn't be any issue with the father because this was the plan we agreed to all along. Since the RDP legislation there wasn't any issue with us doing this, thank goodness.

Several other lesbians who had children through artificial insemination made similar comments to those made by Anne. Those who had older children from previous marriages also noted that they needed to negotiate similar arrangements with their ex-spouses to ensure that their same-sex partner would have legal guardianship of children in the case of serious injury or death. Sonia, who is from British Columbia and is in a four-year relationship, said:

> When we got together and it became clear that we wanted to be life-partners, we became concerned that our son, Noel, wouldn't

be able to live with Jo if anything happened to me. My husband Scott was already in a new relationship and was newly married, so I had to ask him if he would agree to this. He has a new baby and a new wife and, although he loves Noel, he agreed that if I died he would allow Jo to be his legal parent and guardian. He had to sign some sort of paper to this effect, too. So that makes us feel safer, although we really hope that we are all really old if anything like that happened, so it wouldn't be an issue.

Because most of the respondents were not parents, the issue of who would be responsible for the legal guardianship of dependent children was not frequently discussed.

What Factors Led to Discussions of End-of–Life Issues?

There were many in-depth, interesting, and varied responses to this question. As noted earlier, one of the primary reasons given for engaging in end-of-life discussions involved previous experiences of friends/family and associates after the death of a partner, especially where the surviving partner lost shared assets to biological family members who were either unaware of, or unsupportive of, the relationship. Another reason why such discussions were held had to do with respondents wanting legal and social recognition of their relationships. There was also the desire to discuss matters that would affect how partners grew older together and how each would be cared for if and when the need arose. Several people noted that these discussions began early on in relationships, especially if they were contemplating registering relationships through RDPs or were hoping to obtain a marriage certificate once Parliament legalizes same-sex marriage.

Among those who spoke about previous experiences with the deaths of ex-partners, friends, or associates is Josie, who lives in Nova Scotia and is in a six-year relationship:

We have had conversations about many of these issues — especially about writing wills and powers of attorney — throughout our relationship, beginning when we chose to live together. Many of these conversations about these issues have been prompted by the death of a close friend or someone in our circle of friends or relatives. Part of what prompted us to have these conversations was my own experience in a previous relationship. When I was partnered with S, her chronic illness, and the possibility of a recurrence of breast cancer, prompted us to have a medical power of attorney drawn up so that if anything happened I could make all the necessary decisions. S and I had talked at length about her wishes with respect to quality of life versus being alive. In addition, S was concerned that if something happened to her, her mother would swoop in and make the choices that suited her rather than the choices that S would make for herself. When Liz and I became partners six years ago, we talked about what kinds of things we might need to do in order to ensure that we would/could be able to make choices with and for one another. This is an ongoing conversation.

The notion of family members "swooping in" to make decisions not necessarily in keeping with those of their children or their partners was invoked frequently throughout this research. Len, who is from Ontario and is in a seventeen-year relationship, commented:

While I was in this relationship with Ted one of our best friends died of AIDS. He and his partner of eleven years had not made any of these plans. I guess they thought they would live forever or something. Ross's death was a horrible one, he had all sorts of secondary infections and other aids-related illnesses and so was in and out of hospital all the time. Before the final stages of the disease Art made a lot of decisions about his care, but towards the latter stages Ross's parents came from BC and made it very clear to everyone that they were his next of kin and that they would decide what happened to him. His father, in particular, just swooped in, even going so far as to move into their home, and from there he directed the whole thing. All their friends could do was watch in horror as people who hardly knew him made the decisions for Ross's care. We were certain that that wasn't going to be the case in our relationship, so we had these discussions fairly early on.

Bea, who lives in Nova Scotia and is in a twelve-year relationship, described why she and her partner decided to make end-of-life plans:

> We know of friends who have experienced all kinds of nightmares of biological family members just taking over when someone dies. This is what happened to a friend of ours. They had been together for fourteen years prior to one of them dying from cancer. Of course they were closeted, so the family knew only that they lived together as friends. When Kim became so ill that she had to be hospitalized, her parents flew in from Florida and just organized everything. Her partner and friends just stood by in total horror as we were completely removed from her final days on this earth. It was tragic, and straight away we decided to do something about it for ourselves. Especially as my partner has an ex-husband and kids who might feel they should have some say in what happens at the end of her life.

Caring for elderly family members inside or outside of their relationships also functioned as the catalyst for some respondents to discuss their own wishes regarding end-of-life care. Tony, who is from Ontario and is in a seven-year relationship, discussed the following situation:

> My Dad died a few years ago and my Mum got Alzheimer's, so she had to move in with us. I only have the one sister and she has three kids, so Mum going there wasn't an option. Dad had a will leaving everything to Mum, but she never got around to doing anything about her assets. She is so out of it that she hasn't a clue what she would want done with anything, including her own health. It really made us think about how it would be if one of us got something like Alzheimer's, and how we would want to be sure that the other one was the major beneficiary of everything we had built up together, because of course our "marriage" would not be legal like Mum and Dad's.

Other respondents also spoke of caring for older parents in the latter's homes, and they discussed the fact that they would inherit these premises on the death of the parent. In these circumstances, and especially when other siblings were also in the picture, they wanted to ensure that their partners would be fully covered in the case of serious illness or death. Charlene, who is from Nova Scotia and who has been in a same-sex relationship for a "long, long time," provided the following story:

> My eighty-eight-year-old Mum lives with us in her home. She has said that when she dies I will inherit it, and I plan to leave it to R when I die if I go first. We have lived here since we first got together, so if I died first, even before Mum, then R would be royally screwed and this really bothers us. I did talk to a lawyer about it, but until Mum legally leaves the house to me ... which she isn't going to do right now because she is scared that if she turns it over to me now my brother and sisters would have a fit, and she wants what she calls "harmony" in her old age. So we are in a very scary position right now, and as we get older it is more worrying to us because you never know what could happen. So yes, living with Mum has caused us to have these discussions, but we haven't been able yet to do more than talk about it.

Other factors that caused respondents to discuss end-of-life decisions concerned wanting to know that their affairs were in order. Kate, who is from Nova Scotia and is in a seven-year relationship, put it succinctly: "We were planning to buy property together and it seemed the most logical thing to do, to ensure that everything was taken care of, it was as simple as that."

Some respondents chose to have end-of-life discussions when they came out. They saw it as part of their opportunity to affirm public recognition of their relationships and of their responsibilities to each other. According to Elaine and Jo, who are from Nova Scotia and are in a twenty-year relationship: "We came out of the closet and we knew we wanted to publicly take care of each other and have that recognized by our friends and family." While Stuart, who is also from Nova Scotia and who is in a ten-year relationship, noted: "Our commitment ceremony caused us to have these discussions because we wanted in it to indicate that we were more than just 'friends,' and because families can be difficult in times of crisis, especially when faced with illness or death."

Several informants talked about the fact that their own aging caused them to discuss end-of-life-issues not only for themselves but also for family members and friends for whom they either cared or observed needing care. Pete, who is from British Columbia and who is in a fourteen-year relationship, discussed using getting older as an "excuse" for having end-of-life discussions:

> Getting older certainly gave us the excuse for talking about these things — that and accumulating wealth, hearing about other gay couples having problems with family members who became uncooperative after death. When we were younger these topics didn't seem important. The older I get the more I see them as essential things to talk about.

Ted, who is from Ontario and is in a three-year relationship with a "much younger man" also invoked the notion of age: "From the beginning we promised to look after each other, and talking about these important topics, especially in light of our age differences, is part of doing just that." Liz, who is from British Columbia and is in an eighteen-year relationship, was clear about the importance of discussing these topics and acknowledged that she and her partner had done so. She nonetheless acceded that, "with the exception of medical treatment decisions and cremation, we've committed nothing to writing."

Many respondents said that they started to have discussions about end-of-life issues early on in their relationships, usually within the first two years. Zoë lives in Ontario and is in a four-year relationship. She noted that, due to her partner's ill health, they were "propelled into" having such discussions: "When we first got together we started to have these talks because my partner has a chronic health condition that requires medical attention. We wanted to ensure that we both knew what she wanted in the event that it became worse."

As well as a partner's health, another issue raised concerned the health of parents and other relatives. Gwen, who lives in Ontario and is in an eight-year relationship, commented:

> We started these discussions when dealing with these issues with respect to our parents. Also, with L's large immediate family, there were certain issues around burial and medical treatment that

would be contentious if wishes weren't specifically spelled out (in terms of a difference in our religious beliefs). We started talking about these things in our second year together.

A reason given for why respondents had not done anything about end-of-life discussions was the financial inability to do so. Georgina, who lives in Nova Scotia and is in a seven-year relationship, explained her situation as follows:

> Sad to say, although we have discussed all of these documents many times, we have not yet done anything about implementing them. The will made sense as it was until a couple of years ago, as I had minor children who were covered under the terms of the will. Since then, writing a new will is one of those things I/we need to do, but it keeps getting shelved in the process of daily living. Although my partner and I have had many conversations about putting together new wills, powers of attorney, medical treatments, et cetera, we also have not had the income until very recently to effect these legal documents. Now that we are both working, it is probable that we will pursue this aspect more vigorously over the next short while.

A few of those who said that they had not discussed end-of-life issues had not done so because they were not open about their relationships. For example, Joyce, who is from Nova Scotia and is in an eight-year relationship with another woman, put it this way: "Well we don't really have these discussions at all because I am married and we don't want anyone to find out about us. No one knows, and we certainly wouldn't want doctors or nurses or those sorts of people finding out."

In a recent on-line poll conducted in the United States, only 49 percent of gay, lesbian, bisexual, and transgendered people said that they told their physicians about their sexual orientation (Dotinga 2002). To my knowledge, similar research has not been conducted in Canada; if it were to be conducted, however, I suspect that the results would be comparable.

In twenty-five years of teaching courses in the sociology of death and dying, and leading workshops and courses in the community, I have seldom met with groups of people who have made end-of-life decisions. Certainly, students of all ages, especially younger ones, admit that, although they see the need for such discussions with loved ones, they have never put anything in writing. Based on such experiences, it seems to me that the percentage of individuals who have made such decisions is much higher in the gay and lesbian community than it is in the heterosexual community, but I have no empirical data to support this assertion.

Knowledge of the Difficulties
Faced by Other Lesbians and Gay Men

A large number of respondents (63 percent) said that they knew of other lesbians and gay men who had experienced difficulties with end-of-life decisions upon a partner's death. Most respondents alluded to the fact that these problems ensued as a result of families of origin either not knowing about, or not being accepting of, the sexual orientation of the dying or dead person. Three interrelated issues were raised in response to this question: family issues, legal issues, and miscommunication issues. Subsumed within the latter was the issue of couples not making their relationships visible for fear of being outed.

Among those who spoke about family issues as posing difficulties for friends and acquaintances is Beth, who now lives in Nova Scotia and is in a six-year relationship.

> When R died he and T had been cohabiting partners for several years (I think about seven). R's mother was the beneficiary of all his life insurance policies and the executrix and principle benefi-ciary of his estate — that was the way it had always been. R's parents and T were jointly involved in making the funeral arrange-ments, but because the money for same was all coming from the proceeds of R's estate, his mother was the person that the funeral director[s] were dealing with most directly. All through the usual "visitation" period of two days prior to the funeral T and I were at the funeral home along with R's parents and siblings. However, on the day of the funeral, when T and I arrived at the funeral home, we were told by the staffer who greeted us that "none of the family had arrived yet." At the end of the funeral service, the officiating minister invited everyone "on behalf of R's family, to join them for

refreshments at R's home." T was furious and heartbroken, and T's sister, niece, nephew, and I were all appalled by the total erasure of the relationship between T and R.

R trusted his parents to "do what he wanted them to do." I don't think he realized that, although some of his family seemed quite accepting of his relationship with T, they were not prepared to offer that relationship the same kind of value, respect, and priority that they would give a straight relationship. T did not get to stand in the same place as the "grieving widow" — even inside his own house. Even though R's family were civil, I know that they made sure that R's "share" in the cost of the house was paid out in full before they transferred ownership into T's name.

This event had a profound effect on me and the woman who was my partner at the time. Three years later, when S learned that she had a recurrence of breast cancer, which has metastasized to her liver, she started making plans for her funeral, and we made sure that I was her executrix and "principal mourner."

Many others related similar stories. For example, Tess, who lives in Nova Scotia and is in an eight-year relationship, told me the following:

> When my best friend's partner of twenty-three years died, his parents intervened in the whole thing, even to the extent of not allowing his partner to be in the hospital room. They told the nurses not to let him in. They made all the funeral arrangements and even tried to go to court to take their house away. Of course they should have made wills, but as they were in the closet they didn't want anyone to know.

Joy also lives in Nova Scotia, and she is in a ten-and-a-half-year relationship. She discussed the fears she and her partner had when they first came out to her partner's children: "We were particularly concerned because my partner's family was antagonistic towards me. Now, however, they seem to have made a huge turnaround, which lowers our concern. My partner's children are very supportive and would, we believe, not interfere in any arrangements I make concerning my partner."

Peter, who lives in Ontario and is in a fourteen-year relationship, told me about his friend who, when his partner was dying, was not "allowed in the hospital room by E's parents. As well, his partner ended up with nothing, with no will or anything. The law apparently gives everything to the family of origin, regardless of the relationship which existed between them."

Vicki and Jill, who live in Nova Scotia and who have been in a relationship for the past six and a half years, told a story about a friend who had committed suicide:

> A friend of ours committed suicide. The family did not recognize her life as a lesbian, they excluded her friends from the funeral, they wouldn't let us visit her grave or attend the church service. They wanted to cover up who she was as a human being. Their silence kept her in the closet.

Ted, who is from Ontario and is in a three-year relationship, provided yet another version of the same story — a story that I heard over and over — about families who would not allow their child's partner to play an active role in the organization of death rituals.

> I know of many horror stories from my past, especially when going to funerals. One in particular stands out. The couple had been together for thirty years and the deceased's family would not allow the partner to sit with them in either the funeral home chapel or the church. He stood at the back of the chapel like a stranger. I went (with many friends) and stood with him. I felt it was outrageous and unchristian for them to ignore the lover. It was a catholic ceremony and I remember the priest kept referring to the deceased using another name. It almost made me feel I was at the wrong funeral. None of my friends or his lover ever used that name, it was very surreal.

If ever there was a reason for lesbians and gay men to make end-of-life decisions, it seems to me that these stories, and the many others that were told to me, are that reason.

Legal issues often came up in response to the question about whether or not respondents had read or heard about others having difficulties after the death of a partner. According to Angie, who lives in Nova Scotia and who is in a six-year relationship:

> We have known many gay and lesbian couples who have been dragged through the courts over transfer of property, shared child parenting, and transfer of pensions, and so on. It is very depressing. A friend of ours is one of those currently taking the government to court in a joint class action because they did not allow him to receive his partner's pension when he died about eight years ago. After his partner's death due to AIDS, his lifestyle changed completely. And now that he has the virus himself he needs all the support he can get.

Tina, who is also from Nova Scotia and who has been in a same-sex relationship since 1991, had a similar experience with a friend who had been in a twelve-year relationship and died suddenly due to heart failure. Even though she and her partner owned a house and a summer cottage, both of them were in her name because she had borrowed the money from the bank to secure a mortgage and they chose not to make their relationship public. Tina's friend, Wanda, died without a will or any other legal document identifying her partner as co-owner of the properties. Consequently, when she died,

> it was a really negative experience. They weren't out of the closet so the family didn't know, and they made all the arrangements to sell the house and the cottage as well as all the furniture and special things they had collected together. They also made all the funeral arrangements and decided who should be invited and who would get what. We tried to tell Val to tell them about their relationship, but she was too cut up herself and Wanda had never said that they could tell her parents so Val though it was a betrayal to tell them. It was a really tragic situation, and it goes to show that you never know what could happen so you should be prepared.

Calli, who lives in British Columbia and who is in a sixteen-year relationship, added an interesting dimension to her response to this question. She said that she had known many lesbians and gay men who had

lost property, savings, possessions, pets, cars, and other personal belongings after the death of a partner because they had not made end-of-life
decisions. She concluded that the need to make such decisions is "vital. It
is crucial to make directions and complete such tasks because it helps the
surviving partner cope with the loss and the process of grieving. It may be
the last loving gift one can leave their partner."

In order to deal with loss and to go through the grief process it is
important to have the time, energy, and resources to manage one's life
without one's life-partner. Such a loss is devastating for most people,
regardless of how long they have been in the relationship. Knowing that
affairs are in order not only helps the dying person come to terms with her
or his own death but also helps those who are left behind.

Being in the closet is detrimental to enabling lesbian and gay couples
to be open about their relationships and, thus, their end-of-life choices.
Even so, many choose to remain in the closet for fear of being ostracized
by family, friends, acquaintances, employers, and others. And this leads
to endless issues of miscommunication. Consider the case of Dennis, who
lives in Nova Scotia and who is in a nine-year relationship:

> We have friends who are businessmen; they are not out and are
> very fearful of their community finding out about them. They
> were both previously married and Ken has two kids. They don't
> want anyone to know about them, except their closest friends.
> And somehow, because they don't communicate their relation-
> ship outside of that tiny group, they don't communicate these
> things with each other either. When we did the RDP we tried to get
> them to talk about doing wills and estate planning. We told them
> we might be able to get a deal if we all did them at the same time.
> But because they are so closeted they are terrified that someone
> outside of their friendship group will find out. It is a very sad
> situation, but you have to let people do their own thing.

Another example of people not adequately communicating their wishes
for end-of-life care was provided by Beth, who is from Ontario and is in a
four-year relationship:

> When I was with my ex we were very closeted; we were together

for sixteen years and not a soul knew. We didn't have gay friends and we were careful about how we acted around each other in public. When we split up we had a hell of a time figuring out who should get what because the house was in her name so no one would know we bought it together. She was a high school principal and had a huge hang-up about people finding out. Anyway, then she got together with another woman and that woman got cancer and they didn't do wills or anything. When her lover was really sick she wanted to have home care and die at home, but G wouldn't hear of it because people would find out about them. They never communicated any of their fears about death, the final arrangements for the funeral and stuff. Nothing like that at all.

As long as lesbians and gay men continue to live with the fear of homophobia they will continue to be careful about making their relationships visible and public. Even though there is some social acceptance of our relationships, there is still a very long way to go before we achieve the recognition that is accorded heterosexual couples.

Is It Important to Make End-of-Life Decisions?

Ninety-seven percent of the respondents said that making end-of-life decisions was important; the remaining 3 percent did not answer the question. As we have seen, those who did respond provided a variety of reasons for making end-of-life decisions. Most invoked the lack of legal recognition of same-sex relationships as making it particularly important for lesbians and gay men to make such decisions.

Recognizing the need for making legal decisions about end-of-life eventualities, Joanne, who is from British Columbia and who is in a three-year relationship, said: "Because we lack the legal status of opposite sex couples I would say these decisions are vital to our relationships. Especially in our case, as we have a child and we want to ensure that he is well taken care of." Similarly, Lisa, who is from Nova Scotia and who is in a seven-year relationship, said:

I think it is important for any couple to have these conversations; further to this, it seems to me to be a pressing issue that same-sex couples not only have these conversations but also get all of the legal paperwork in place to ensure that their wishes, [as] individual[s] and as a couple, are followed.

Ironically, even though Lisa is very clear about the need for such discussions to occur and to be formally implemented, she also notes: "I know that we haven't done any of this, but that doesn't change the fact that I believe it is important!"

Jess, who is from New Brunswick and is in a two-year relationship, also noted the special need for lesbians and gay men to make end-of–life decisions:

> It is important for personal peace of mind and understanding [for everyone]. Also, same-sex couples have to plan for end of life more so than heterosexual couples, in light of the added legal documents required [even RDPs do not provide those registered with the rights/obligations of married couples under estate and intestate legislation].

Brenda, who is from Nova Scotia and is in a six-year relationship, raised the issue of the financial costs of making end-of-life decisions as a lesbian couple:

> Apparently we don't have full human rights in this country to be able to name our spouses, like all other adults can do, and therefore must take extraordinary and expensive measures to *make* happen what is considered automatic for heterosexual couples. When my partner was married to a man, it was naturally assumed that when he or she died, everything would go to the other partner. We do not have the same privileges as lesbians or gay men.

A theme often raised concerned the need to ensure that each partner's final wishes were met. Jane, who is from Nova Scotia and is in a fourteen-and-a-half-year relationship, remarked:

> People often get greedy and selfish when someone dies, and they think they deserve and have the right to make final decisions and

have ownership of the deceased person's possessions. So one must protect themselves with any legal methods available. It also makes life easier for the surviving spouse/children [because] you know what the deceased person's wishes are and you don't have to guess.

Many people were concerned that if we didn't ensure that our personal end-of-life wishes were are met, then someone else would. Nina, who is from Ontario and is in a seven-and-a-half-year relationship, raised this issue:

My feeling is that we need to do this for ourselves as a couple because if we don't then someone else, probably our families, will do it for us; and it is doubtful that they will know, or maybe even care about, our wishes. I think it is absolutely essential that we take control and get the outcome which we want, especially in a society where our rights are not yet secure.

Vicky and Jill, who are living in Nova Scotia and are in a six-and-a-half-year relationship, agreed with Nina's sentiment:

Absolutely! It is urgent that we demand our legal rights and push for relationship/family recognition. We need to know that, in the eventual death of a partner, we will have all the support and resources available to us during this time of great loss. Further, we want our families to stand beside us and not against us when the time comes for us to die.

Jamie, who is from Ontario and is in a nine-year relationship, talked about not wanting to "second guess" his partner's end-of-life wishes:

My goodness, yes, we do have to have these discussions; and when we have been clear about what we would like we need to put it in writing and give it to our lawyers, doctors, family, and friends. You have enough to grieve about when your partner dies without having to worry about whether or not you did the right thing by them at the end.

The notion of second guessing was also raised by Valerie, who is from Nova Scotia and is in a seven-year relationship:

> Yes, it is important for same-sex couples to make end-of-life decisions — absolutely — because I think it is important that everyone do this and communicate those decisions to the people who matter in their lives. Dying and death is a highly emotionally charged time. The more that is already in place and communicated the easier it is for everyone. They don't have to second guess your wishes or argue over what you "might have wanted to happen." I was out visiting my parents over Christmas (they are in their eighties), and they really wanted to sit down and talk with me and show me all the arrangements they have made regarding their deaths. They have the plots, the stones, everything paid for: my brother and I know that everything is divided evenly between us and that they would like 10 percent to go to their church. They showed me where their wills and papers are. They are facing the prospect of their own deaths but are doing so in a way that reflects how they have lived — organized, thoughtfully, and [with] every-one know[ing] what they want. That's the way it should be. Taking care of dying is just part of taking care of living.

Death is part of life: no one escapes it, and it doesn't matter whether we are straight, gay or lesbian, bisexual, transgendered, or any combination thereof over any given lifetime. We will all die. If we want to ensure that our final time on earth is what we want it to be — assuming that we do not die in an accident or as the result of a violent act committed by ourselves (suicide) or by another (war/murder), then we must make plans with those we love. If we want to support our partners in their grief process by discussing with them our final wishes, then we shall die more peacefully knowing that we have had the opportunity to share these crucial decisions.

Suggested Additions
When I asked respondents if they had anything they wanted to add to the questionnaire, only 14 percent mentioned substantive issues. Lorraine, who is living in Ontario and is in a four-year relationship, said: "I would

be very interested in knowing if couples have discussion about grief-dealing strategies. You know who to turn to for help dealing with grief and that sort of thing." Zoe, who lives in Nova Scotia and is in a seven-year relationship, questioned whether or not the state has any role in determining end-of-life decisions:

> Really, I think end-of-life decisions are the same as any other type of relationship decision. The people who talk about things will talk about them. Those that don't, don't. The people who organize the details of their lives organize them. Those who don't, don't. I think rather than turning to the state to fix up our problems and disputes after we're dead, we should live consciously, which means dealing with things — not just financially and legally. But really, it is more about communicating — with your partner, your family, those who matter in your life.
>
> If you have the type of family/people in your life who get crazy or have issues over money it is important to deal with it before it becomes a problem, and the more you plan the less there is to deal with. For same-sex couples there have been fewer imposed rules, and I think that is a good thing. Do I care that my partner will have to pay income tax on my estate and opposite-sex partners don't? If I did, I have the choice of registering for the RDP. It just doesn't matter enough to me to give up the autonomy of defining my relationship as we choose.

Bett, who lives in Nova Scotia and is in a six-year relationship, thought that it was particularly important for *Passing Through* "to document how really *angry* we are becoming about being deprived of basic human rights as individuals and as couples."

A few respondents thought that the book should address prenuptial type contracts for partners who are planning either to marry or to become registered. For example, Shane, who lives in Ontario and is in a three-year relationship, said:

> I think that you should talk about prenuptial type contracts between couples. We have one, and, although we want to get married as soon as the law is changed, I want to ensure that I don't

lose my business if our relationship ever broke up. I think that more gay men are careful about this than lesbians.

Brad, who is also from Ontario and who is in a twelve-year relationship, commented:

> We plan to either get the RDP (if it ever comes to Toronto) or to marry, whichever comes first. In the meantime we have a prenuptial agreement in place which ensures that if we split up (which I hope we never do) that we each get back what we put into the relationship. It just seems sensible to me to take these precautions, and it is something that gays and lesbians need to know that they can do.

Interestingly enough, none of the lesbians in the study addressed this issue.

A few respondents, such as Jess (who is from New Brunswick and is in a two-year relationship), suggested that it would have been useful if I had asked whether people were "out" about their relationships as this would affect their ability to have discussions with service-providers regarding end-of-life decisions. Sam, who is from Ontario and is in an eight-year relationship, framed this suggestion slightly differently:

> I would be very interested in knowing how many gay men and lesbians are still in the closet, because this would have a bearing on how comfortable they felt about talking with the people who count — like doctors, nurses, funeral directors, lawyers, bankers, et cetera — about end-of-life decisions. Obviously, if they don't want anyone to know they are gay then how can anyone help them with these issues?

An interesting suggestion was raised by Nan, who lives in Nova Scotia and is in a ten-and-a-half-year relationship:

> I think you should point out how important it is to have good relationships with the local funeral homes. I have attended funerals where all the pallbearers were women, much to the surprise of the

funeral director! I would suggest that visiting the funeral homes nearby while you are still alive and kicking is a very good idea.

Interestingly, in spite of Nan's suggestion, no respondents discussed the notion of pre-planning their funerals or cremations as a way of ensuring that their wishes for final disposition were met. There could be a number of reasons for this. For one thing, I assume that the funeral industry is not doing a very good job of targetting lesbians and gay men, or even younger people, as most of their material is aimed at older, heterosexual persons. For another, the fear of dying inhibits many people, thus keeping them from making the kinds of decisions they need to make. And, of course, systemic homophobia ensures that many lesbians and gay men remain in the closet, thus preventing them from making appropriate plans for final disposition.

Ben and Jock, who are from Nova Scotia and are in a seventeen-year relationship, suggested I mention long-term care and critical illness insurance policies. Because these have recently been included in basic life-insurance coverage I did not mention them in the questionnaire. However, as they gain recognition and acceptability, I hope that more lesbians and gay men will include them in their insurance plans, especially when considering later life care needs.

Chapter Six

What Should You Do?

What an interesting, enjoyable, and enlightening experience this has been — except, of course, for the parliamentary commission and the current debate around same-sex marriage, in which homophobia abounds. It is clear to me from having conducted this research that lesbians and gay men have very conscientiously and thoughtfully made end-of-life plans and that these topics are discussed in the lesbian and gay community, at least among older persons. Why is it that a seemingly disproportionate number of lesbians and gay men have made end-of-life decisions? I think that the answer lies in some of the following observations:

1. Due to the tremendous number of deaths due to HIV/AIDS in the gay community, everyone knows someone who has been affected by the virus and its aftermath. Although, according to Health AIDS Canada (<http://www.hc-sc.gc.ca/english/women/facts_issues/facts_aids.htm/women_e.html>), lesbians are not presently in a high-risk group, many have worked within AIDS organizations and have friends who have died of AIDS.

2. Due to their fear of homophobia, many people are not yet open about their relationships. This experience not only robs them of the possibility of publicly expressing their grief but it also tells others in the lesbian and gay communities that this could happen to them if they are not open about their relationships.

3. It is common knowledge within the lesbian and gay communities that, if legal decisions are not in place, those families who are not comfortable with the sexual orientation of their loved ones tend to "take over" decisions and arrangements prior to, during, and after death.

4. Within the lesbian and gay communities free estate planning and will

preparation courses are available, albeit predominantly in the urban areas. Organizations such as EGALE Canada also provide information on these topics if requested, as will Lambda in the United States.

5. Those who choose to register their relationships or hold commitment ceremonies often use those occasions to make end-of-life decisions and arrangements, thus helping these topics to become visible and common-place within our communities.

6. The lack of legal recognition for same-sex partners ensures that we need to make our final wishes known. If we do not, then biological next-of-kin become the "normal" beneficiaries of wills and estates.

If you haven't made end-of-life decisions, the following sections will tell you what you need to know and do.

Legal Wills

Ensure that you have a will, a living will, and a health guardian or similar proxy. Although will forms are available it is more appropriate to seek the services of a lawyer, especially if children are involved. Each province in Canada has regulations regarding the disposition of a person's estate after death, and there are also provincial guidelines describing what form of will is acceptable. While British Columbia is the only province that officially requires a typed will, all provinces prefer them to hand-written wills (check with a lawyer or legal advisor to determine your province's precise preference).

The purpose of a will is straightforward: it states what an individual wants to happen with her or his assets (i.e., who gets what, when, and under what conditions). A will may also indicate your wishes regarding funeral arrangements and who will care for children should you predecease them. It may be used to document your wishes regarding the provisions you want to make for minor dependants in the event of your death, and it may include last words of comfort to specific family members and friends. If you do not have a will, intestate laws dictate that your biological family will inherit all of your possessions. Not only does a legal will allow you to say who gets what when, but it also gives you permission to indicate whom you *do not* want to receive your assets or belongings (similarly, a living will allows you to notify your health care providers as to whom you do not want making decisions that directly affect your health).

The issue of living wills and advanced health care directives is separate from but connected with those issues involving the right to die with dignity; the right to refuse treatment even if such refusal could result in an earlier death; the rights of the mentally challenged or incompetent adult patient; and the criteria for the determination of death, euthanasia, and assisted suicide as well as the civil and criminal liabilities of health care professionals. With so many interwoven legal, personal, and professional interests, it is clear that living wills and medical directives represent an interesting legal challenge and that they have a very real impact on social, political, religious, and medical practices and decisions surrounding the end of life.

Advanced Health Care Directives

Although living wills are not legally binding in Canada, many provinces recognize advanced health care directives. In a ground-breaking Canadian booklet entitled *Let Me Decide*, Molloy and Mepham (1992) note that there are two types of advance directives other than a will or power of attorney: an instructional directive and a proxy directive. Molloy and Mepham differentiate between these directives as follows: "An instructional directive states which treatments are wanted or not wanted under any given circumstances. These statements can be as general or specific as desired. But the more specific they are, the easier for the family and doctors to follow (7). A proxy directive, on the other hand, nominates another person (the proxy or advocate) to make decisions regarding your health care should you become incompetent: "This advocate will have the ability to make health care decisions in much the same way as a power of attorney does for financial matters." (8).

What follows is a copy of the health care directive used by Dr. W. Molloy:

PERSONAL HEALTH CARE DIRECTIVE

I. *Introduction*

In this Directive I have stated my wishes for my own health care should the time ever come when I am not able to communicate because of illness or injury. This Directive should never be used if I am able to decide for myself. It must never be substituted for my judgement if I am competent to make these decisions.

If the time comes when I am unable to make these decisions, I would like this Directive to be followed and respected. In an emergency, please contact my advocate(s) or my family doctor, listed below. If these people are not available, then please do as I have requested in this Directive. Thank you.

I have thought about and discussed my decision with my family, friends and my family doctor. I do not want to leave these decisions to my family, my doctor or strangers who do not know me.

Dated this _____ day of _____ , _____

Signature _____

Print Name _____

Health Insurance Number _____

Copyright © Dr. D.W. Molloy

ADVOCATE(S) and FAMILY PHYSICIAN

Advocate #1

Name _____

Address _____

Home Tel. # _____ Office Tel. # _____

Advocate #2

Name _____

Address _____

Home Tel. # _____ Office Tel. # _____

Family Physcian

Name _____

Address _____

Home Tel. # _____ Office Tel. # _____

II. *Personal Health Care Chart*

This chart is to be consulted only if I am no longer able to make or communicate my own decisions.

My choices are noted in the spaces provided below each section.

III. Definitions of terms used in the Directive

Reversible Condition: Condition that may be cured without any remaining disability; e.g. pneumonia, bleeding ulcers.

Irreversible Condition: Condition that will leave lasting disabilities; e.g. multiple sclerosis, stroke, severe head injury, Alzheimer's disease.

Palliative Care
- keep me warm, dry, and pain-free
- do not transfer to hospital unless absolutely necessary
- only give measures that enhance comfort or minimize pain; e.g., morphine for pain
- intravenous line started only if it improves comfort; e.g., for hydration
- no x-rays, blood tests or antibiotics unless they are given to improve comfort

Limited Care (includes Palliative)
- may or may not transfer to hospital
- intravenous therapy may be appropriate
- antibiotics should be used sparingly
- a trial of appropriate drugs may be used
- no invasive procedures; e.g., surgery
- do not transfer to Intensive Care Unit

Surgical Care (includes Limited)
- transfer to acute care hospital (where patient may be evaluated)
- emergency surgery if necessary
- do not admit to Intensive Care Unit
- do not ventilate (except during and after surgery); i.e., tube down throat and connected with machine

Intensive Care (includes Surgical)
- transfer to acute-care hospital without hesitation
- admit to Intensive Care Unit if necessary
- ventilate if necessary
- insert central line; i.e., main arteries for fluids when other veins collapse

- provide surgery, biopsies, all life-support systems and transfer surgery
- do everything possible to maintain life

Basic Feeding: Spoon feed with regular diet. Give all fluids by mouth that can be tolerated, but make no attempt to feed by special diets, intravenous fluids or tubes.

Supplemental Feeding: Give supplements or special diets, for example, high calorie, fat or protein supplements.

Intravenous Feeding: Give nutrients (water, salt, carbohydrate, protein and fat) by intravenous infusions.

Tube Feed: Use tube feeding. There are two main types:
1. Nasogastric Tube: a soft plastic tube passed through the nose or mouth into the stomach
2. Gastrostomy Tube: a soft plastic tube passed directly into stomach through the skin over the abdomen.

No CPR: Make no attempt to resuscitate.

CPR: Use cardiac massages with mouth-to-mouth breathing; may also include intravenous lines, electric shocks to the heart (defibrillators), tubes in throat to lungs (endotrachial tubes).

V. Personal Statement
I consider an irreversible condition to be any condition

_____

I agree to the following procedures: (write Yes or No)

Post Mortem _____   Blood Transfusion _____

Organ Donation _____   Cremation: _____

Copyright © Dr. D.W. Molloy (1992)

Health Care Proxies/Advance Directives

In appointing a health care proxy, you may appoint a partner, friend, or family member to make health care decisions for you in the event that you are unable to do so yourself.

Powers of Attorney

Appointing someone as your power of attorney allows her/him to act as your representative. She/he may act on your behalf in legal or financial matters if you are unable to do so.

Organ Donations

Most Canadian provinces have their own version of an anatomical gift act, which determines the donation procedures for organs, tissue, blood products, other body parts, and even entire cadavers. Most provinces require donors to sign a specific section of their driver's licence, while others have a separate attachment.

The time factor is crucial in most organ transplants, therefore, except for cornea and skin transplants, hospital deaths are favoured. It should be noted that many medical schools already have sufficient bodies for study (Houlihan 1988). Unfortunately, gay men are presently unable to donate organs (see Chapter 5).

Financial Planning

Making financial plans for the disposition of an estate prior to death can help the executor/executrix to administer it in accordance with the individual's wishes. There are a variety of tax and other legal considerations. Along with financial planning many Canadians also prefer to make pre-paid arrangements for their funerals, again to save their bereaved loved ones from having to perform this difficult task. Most provinces have memorial societies, funeral cooperatives, and other groups that provide lower-cost or pre-paid services.

Preparing Your Own Death Plan

It is common for many Canadian women, when planning to give birth, to produce a detailed plan to assist themselves and their caregivers. For the past eight years, while teaching a course in the sociology of death and dying, I have required students to complete a death plan. This assignment's objective is to enable the student to see what it means to take personal responsibility for our final days as well as for our funeral or memorial services.

The death plan might include place of death; with whom we choose to die (or whether we choose to die alone); whether or not we want medication or pain control; and what happens after our death. The latter includes all the elements of a funeral or memorial service, from music, to flowers, to food and drink, and so on. It includes who, if anyone, would be pallbearers or speakers at the memorial service (if there is one), and who would preside at the interment (if there is one).

Most students find this a fascinating and rewarding exercise. Many include letters to important ones saying their final goodbyes, write poems, or select songs they want presented at their wakes. This assignment brings death closer to home and helps them realize how much work is involved in making final decisions. It helps them to take some responsibility for tying up loose ends.

When completing all legal documents that have a bearing on end-of-life issues, it is necessary to provide copies to our partners, family (including children, if applicable), spiritual advisors or clergy (if applicable), funeral director (if pre-planning), physician and other health care providers, and (of course) our lawyers. Presenting such documentation to the important people in our lives, and to those who provide services to us, also allows the topic of end-of-life care to be brought out in the open and freely discussed. Consequently, if disagreements or confusion arises, then they can be addressed.

It is important for everyone to discuss and document their wishes with regard to end-of-life care. But it is especially important for lesbians and gay men to do so. It is the only way that we can enjoy our lives without having to be afraid of what might happen to our partners, ourselves, and other loved ones once we have finally "passed through."

Appendix

Passing Through:
The End-of-Life Decisions of Lesbians and Gay Men

Jeanette A. Auger
36 Pleasant Street
Wolfville, NS, B4P IM7
Tel: (902) 542-4234
E-mail: jeanetteaauger@ns.sympatico.ca

Preamble

I am writing a book (to be published by Fernwood Publishing in Halifax later this year) about the end-of-life decisions made by same-sex partners. I am particularly interested in knowing whether such decisions have been made and, if so, whether (and how) they have been affected by the new registered domestic partnership (RDP) legislation. To date, RDP legislation has been passed in Nova Scotia, Quebec, and Manitoba. Theoretically, with the exception of the right to marry, this legislation gives us the same rights and obligations as those held by common-law couples. I am conducting a series of focus groups and surveys aimed at finding out what arrangements our community members have made for end-of-life decisions, and I thank you for your input.

If you are responding by mail, please feel free to use additional sheets.
Your responses will remain confidential.

Name(s) _____

_____

Age(s) _____

Are you in a same-sex relationship?   Yes   No   N/A
If so, for how long? _____

Have you officially registered
your relationship (RDP)?   Yes   No   N/A

If so, why? If not, why not? _____

_____

Do you have any of the following (and when did you acquire it)?

Will	Yes	No	N/A
Living will	Yes	No	N/A
Medical directive	Yes	No	N/A
Power of attorney	Yes	No	N/A
Life insurance	Yes	No	N/A
Joint accounts	Yes	No	N/A
Joint ownership of property	Yes	No	N/A

Why did you decide to obtain or not to obtain the above, and why?

_____

_____

As a couple have you discussed the following?

Medical treatment decisions	Yes	No	N/A
Funeral/cremation/burial wishes	Yes	No	N/A
Services regarding the above	Yes	No	N/A
Where you want to die (at home, in a hospital, palliative care unit, hospice, rest home, other?)	Yes	No	N/A
Organ donations	Yes	No	N/A
Estate planning and investments	Yes	No	N/A
If you have children have you appointed your partner as legal guardian should you predecease her/him?	Yes	No	N/A

If not, why not? _____

_____

What factors caused you to have the above discussions? And at approximately what point in your relationship did they occur? _____

_____

_____

Have you heard or read about other lesbians and gay men having difficulties with any of the above after the death of a partner?   Yes   No   N/A

If so, what happened? _____

_____

Do you think it is important for same-sex
couples to make end-of-life decisions?   Yes   No   N/A
If so, why? If not, why not? _____

_____

Is there anything that you would add
to this questionnaire or that you think
should be included in the book?   Yes   No   N/A
If so, what? _____

_____

Thank you for participating in this research.

References

Ambert, Ann-Marie. 2003. *Same-Sex Couples and Same-Sex Parent Families: Relationships, Parenting, and Issues of Marriage. Ottawa: Vanier Institute of the Family.* Available on-line at <http://www.vifamily.ca/library/cft/samesex.html>

Baker, Maureen. 1984. *The Family: Changing Trends in Canada.* Toronto: McGraw Hill.

Bernard, Jessie. 1972. *The Future of Marriage.* New York. Bantam.

Bohan, J.S. 1996. *Psychology and Sexual Orientation: Coming to Terms.* New York: Routledge.

Brotman, Shari, Bill Ryan, and Robert Cormier. 2003. "Discrimination Threatens Gay Elders' Health." *Gerontologist* 43 (April):192-202.

Canada Customs and Revenue Agency. 2000. *Modernizing the Treatment of Personal Relationships in Federal Legislation: Same-Sex Partners and Tax Legislation.* <http://www.ccra-adrc.gc.ca/tax/individuals/faq/same_sex-e.html>

Compas Opinion and Market Research. 2000. "Homosexuality and Bisexuality: Third Annual Sun/COMAS Sex Survey." *Toronto Sun,* 23 September.

Canada. Department of Justice. 2000. *Backgrounder: Modernization of Benefits and Obligations.* <http://canada.justice.gc.ca/en/news/nr/2000/doc_25021.html>.

Demczuk, Irene, Michele Caron, Ruth Rose, and Lyne Bouchard. 2002. *Recognition of Lesbian Couples: An Inalienable Right.* Ottawa: Status of Women Canada

Doka, Kenneth. J. 1989. *Disenfranchised Grief: Recognizing Hidden Sorrow.* New York: Lexington.

Dotinga, Randy. 2002. *Many Hide GLBT Orientation from Doctors.* <http://uk.gay.com/headlines/3253>. 19 December.

Faulkner, Anne H., and Kevin Cranston. 1998. "Correlates of Same-Sex Sexual Behavior in a Random Samples of Massachusetts High School Students." *Journal of Public Health* 88 (February): 262-66.

findley, barbara. 1997. "All in the Family Values." *Canadian Journal of Family Law* 14: 129-96.

Fisher, John, Kathy Lahey, and Laurie Arron. 2000. *Division of Powers and Jurisdictional Issues Relation to Marriage.* Ottawa: EGALE.

Gewirtzman, Doni. 2000. Advance Planning: Easier Than You Think. Lambda Legal on-line at <http://www.lambdalegal.org/cgi-bin/iowa/documents/record?record=5 >.

Glenn, Evelyn N. 1987. "Gender and the Family." In *Analyzing Gender: A Handbook of Social Science,* ed. Beth H. Hess and Myra Marx Ferree, 237-41. Newbury Park, CA: Sage.

Gordon, Garth. 2001. "Domestic-Partners-Vital Statistics Acts Amendments." Paper presented at the Canadian Bar Association Real Estate/Probate Seminar, Kentville, Nova Scotia, 12 October.

Herman, Didi. 1994. *Rights of Passage: Struggles for Lesbian and Gay Legal Equality.* Toronto: University of Toronto Press.

Houlihan, P.J. 1988. *Life without End: The Transplant Story.* Toronto: NC Press.

How, Lewis H. 2003. "Marriage and the Legal Recognition of Same-Sex Unions." Discussion paper presented to the Standing Committee on Justice and Human Rights, Halifax, Nova Scotia. 7 April.

Hunter, N. 1991. "Marriage, Law and Gender: A Feminist Inquiry." *Law and Sexuality* 9 (1): 23-34.

Kinsey, A.C., W.B. Pomeroy, and C.E. Martin. 1948. *Sexual Behavior in the Human Male.* Philadelphia: W.B. Saunders.

Lahey, Kathleen. 1999. *Are We Persons Yet? Law and Sexuality in Canada.* Toronto: University of Toronto Press.

Lambda Legal Defense and Education Fund. 2002. *Registering As Domestic Partners.*
Los Angeles: Lambda Legal Defense and Education Fund.

Law Commission of Canada. 2002. *Beyond Conjugality: Recognizing and Supporting Close Personal Adult Relationships.* Ottawa: Department of Justice Canada.

Lunman, Kim. 2003. "Ottawa Backs Marriage." *Globe and Mail*, 18 June, 1.

Makin, Kirk. 2003. "Gay Marriage Legalized." *Globe and Mail*, 11 June, 1.

Martin, D.K., E.C.Thiel, and P.A. Singer. 2002. "A New Model of Advance Care Planning: Observations from People with HIV." *Archives of Internal Medicine* (March): 135-39.

McDaniel, Susan A., and Lorne Tepperman. 2000. *Close Relations: An Introduction to the Sociology of Families.* Scarborough, ON: Prentice-Hall Allyn and Bacon.

Mellet, Cathy J. 2003. "An Engaged Dialogue Regarding the Changing Environment of Rights, Obligations and Relationships in the Settlement of Property and Family Conflicts on Lesbians in Halifax." MA thesis, Royal Roads University, Victoria, British Columbia.

Merin, Yuval. 2002. *Equality for Same-Sex Couples*. Chicago: University of Chicago Press.

Michael, Robert, John. H. Gagnon, Edward O. Lauman, and Gina Lokata. 1994. *Sex in America: A Definitive Study*. Boston: Little, Brown.

Molloy, William, and Virginia Mepham. 1992. *Let Me Decide*. Toronto: Penguin.

Money, J. 1988. *Gay, Straight and In-Between: The Sexology of Erotic Orientation*. New York: Oxford University Press.

O'Brien, Carol-Anne, and Lorna Weir. 1995. "Lesbians and Gay Men Inside and Outside of Families." In *Canadian Families*, ed. Nancy Mandell and Ann Duffy, 111-39. Toronto: Harcourt, Brace.

Pina, Darlene, and Vern Bengston. 1995. "Division of Household Labor and the Well-Being of Retirement-Age Wives." *Gerontologist* 35 (June): 237-43.

Rogusky, Derek. 2003. "Marriage Is Debased." *Globe and Mail*, 11 June, A17.

Russell, P. 1995. *The Gay 100: A Ranking of the Most Influential Gay Men and Lesbians, Past and Present*. New York: Citadel.

Sandoval. Nena. 2003. "Brief on the Issue of Same-Sex Marriages in Canada." Presented to the Standing Committee on Justice and Human Rights. Halifax, Nova Scotia. 7 April.

Schumm, Walter, Anthony Jurich, Stephan Ballman, and Margaret Bugaighid. 1996. "His and Her Marriage Revisited." *Journal of Family Issues* 6 (2): 221-27.

Singer, Peter. 1995. "Advance Directive Fallacies." *Health Law In Canada* 16 (1): 5-9

Singer, Peter, Douglas Martin, and Merrijoy Kelner. 1999. "Quality End-of-Life Care: Patient's Perspectives." *Journal of the American Medical Association* 158: 168-79.

Singer, P.A., E.C. Thiel, I. Salit, W. Flanagan, and C.D. Naylor. 1997. "The HIV-Specific Advance Directive." *Journal of General Internal Medicine*. 12: 729-35.

Small, Judy. 1999. "No Tears for the Widow." Words and Music by Judy Small. From the Compact Diskette *Let the Rainbow Shine*. Crafty Maid Music, Victoria, Australia.

Sui, Jack. 2003a. *Canada to Count Gay Heads*. 365Gay.com/NewscenterContent. Toronto Bureau. 30 January.

—. 2003b. *$400M Gay Class Action Suit Grows*. 365Gay.com/ NewscenterContent. Toronto Bureau. 8 April.

—. 2003c. *Labor Supports Gay Marriage*. 365Gay.com/NewscenterContent. Toronto Bureau. 12 April.

Thompson, Ben. 2002. *Census Gives Sketch of Canadian Gay Families*. 365 Gay.com.Newscenter in Ottawa. 22 October.

Warner Home Box Office. 2000. *If These Walls Could Talk 2*. Los Angeles, California: Warner Time Pictures.

Wintermute, Robert, and Mads Andenaes. 2001. *Legal Recognition of Same Sex Relationships: A Study of National, European and International Law*. Portland, OR: Oxford Hart Publishing.

Wood, Owen. 2002. "The Fight for Gay Rights: Canada Timeline." CBC News Online. 3 September.

About the Author

Jeanette A. Auger teaches sociology at Acadia University in Wolfville, Nova Scotia, where she has lived and worked for the past seventeen years. As well as her academic research and teaching, Jeanette has also been active for the past ten years working with the Victorian Order of Nurses in an attempt to open Atlantic Canada's first free-standing hospice. She works closely in the community with and for older persons and the dying and their important ones. Jeanette has written two previous books — *Social Perspectives on Death and Dying* (2000) and, with Diane Tedford-litle, *From the Inside Looking Out: Competing Ideas about Growing Old* (2002) — both published by Fernwood. She lives in Wolfville with her partner, Susan, and an assortment of animal companions.